SIGNALMAN'S MORNING

To my parents,
who loved Old England
and her Greatest Railway

SIGNALMAN'S MORNING

Adrian Vaughan

AMBERLEY

Come, fill the Cup, and in the Fire of Spring
The Winter Garment of repentance fling:
The Bird of Time has but a little way
To fly – and Lo! the Bird is on the Wing.

The Rubáiyát by Omar Khayyám, trans. Edward FitzGerald, I, vii

First published by John Murray 1981
Reprinted John Murray 1982
Paperback edition John Murray 1983
Pan combined edition paperback 1984

Revised edition Amberley Publishing 2011

Amberley Publishing
The Hill, Stroud
Gloucestershire, GL5 4EP

www.amberleybooks.com

British Library Cataloguing in Publication Data.
A catalogue record for this book is available from the British Library.

ISBN 978 1 4456 0256 1

Typesetting and Origination by Amberley Publishing.
Printed in Great Britain.

Contents

Prologue

I am sitting in my car in the market place at Wantage in early summer 1978. It is midday. The morning started cool and clear under the chestnut trees, progressing to harsh heat, sun hot on black paint, dazzling on the white statue of King Alfred. Close by me the market stalls are full of fruit – curved, long, round, shining, yellow and orange, bright. Assistants shadowy under an awning, customers waiting patiently, unaccustomed eyes in winter-pale faces screwed up against the strong light. Opposite, a red Thames Valley diesel rattles unrhythmically. Mill Street roofs, ochre tiles and sideways chimneys drop crookedly downhill; a fringe of green trees on the ridge behind.

My mind sees beyond the willows on the hill to the railway line three miles away and I recall days more distant than any mileage when 'Castles' ran on steel rails not mirage-like in the hot sun of Now. Stopping trains stopped at sunny silent stations deep in the elm tree fields. But now – no elms, no trains, no stations – only the hot Today sun to remind me of those halcyon days.

I knew the steam-hauled railway for twenty years. I loved its beautiful engines whose rhythms were so innately musical that you can hear a 'Castle' skimming down the Vale of the White Horse in at least three great symphonies; I loved it for its handsome signals and signal boxes, for the homely, farming countryside it ran through, but most of all for its men – patient and understanding, the salt of the earth. Through them I learned the technicalities of railway work and absorbed the intangible spirit of 120 years of tradition. For that I will always be grateful.

For the help I received in writing this book, my thanks are due to the following railwaymen and women: Mrs E. Halford and Mrs H. Strong, David Castle, Sam Loder, Elwyn Richards, Albert Stanley, Sid ('Brush') Tyler, Basil Titchener and H. R. Hayden, Area Administration Officer at Swindon. During the Christmas holidays 1979 my family and I were practically homeless, and the hospitality of several kind friends helped me to finish this book: my parents, Martin and Joy Brown, Paul and Sue Dye, Ken and Pat Fuller, Frances and Camillus Travers, Jane and Jim White – and thanks to my wife, Susan, who suffered all hardships cheerfully. I would like to thank my friend Ivo Peters for his helpful criticism of the book; thanks, too, to my publishers, and in particular to my friend Simon Young for his unstinted help in revising the manuscript.

Finally, I would like to thank all the old-hand railway gentlemen for so generously taking me into their world, teaching me the meaning of railway work, and making work a pleasure.

Adrian Vaughan

ACKNOWLEDGEMENTS FOR THE EDITION OF 2011

Grateful thanks to Mr Philip Shepherd of Aston Cantlow, who was inspired to paint a magnificent picture of Uffington station after reading *Signalman's Morning*. He very generously donated the 30 x 15-inch painting to me, and I am delighted to be able to use the central section of it as the cover of the book that gave him so much pleasure.

And finally, I must thank my editor and friend, Nicola Gale at Amberley Publishing, for her kindness for working so hard to make the book a success.

Adrian Vaughan
Barney
North Norfolk
2011

An ex-South Eastern Railway 4-4-0, Southern Railway No. 9 storms up the hill out of Reading and is seen here approaching Earley station. The engine, the design dating from 1883, is pulling GWR coaches and is probably a Birkenhead to Dover train. These engines had been running over the Reading–Redhill line since 1900 if not before, and they were still storming Earley bank when I was a little lad in 1945. The last one of them was scrapped in 1949. This superb photograph was taken in the late 1920s/early 1930s by a friend of my father's, John Ashman. (John Ashman FRPS. Courtesy of Mike Esau)

Chapter One

First Love

At the age of five I ran away from home. I left my bed late one evening not to go to sea but to a signal box. It was two miles from our house in Earley, Reading, separated by the dark trees of Palmer Park, the London road, Sutton's seed ground and two gasometers. I ran hard all the way, arriving at the foot of the signal box stairs to be greeted by a fox terrier barking furiously. The signalman came to the door of his box and called, 'Who's about?'

'Only me, mister.'

He peered down at me standing dim in the faint light from his windows. 'You'd better come up into the box, sonny, and we'll see what this is all about.' He was very kind, gave me some tea and one of his sandwiches while he asked me where I came from. I explained my great desire to go into a signal box, so he delayed telephoning for the police until he had shown me round his box. Significantly, I cannot remember how I got home but I do remember feeling very pleased with myself and looking forward to another visit.

I had been bewitched by the atmosphere of the railway since the age of three. On Wednesday afternoons my father closed his radio repair shop and took the family for a drive in his Austin Seven, and because of a long-standing family connection with the Great Western Railway, the usual destination was Sonning Cutting. We went to a place where the quiet, unfrequented lane and the railway were level with each other and separated only by a wide, grassy verge. It was the perfect site for a picnic with wild flowers to gather and grass snakes to hunt – and, above all, Great Western trains to watch.

The Southern Railway branch line from Reading to Redhill and Waterloo climbed steeply in a cutting within earshot of our house; the ancient engines labouring heavily up the grade, throwing half-burnt coal and soot out of their chimneys so high that it rose above the roofs of the houses that lined the south side of the cutting's rim and fell smuttily on my aunt's washing. The incline passed by 'Solly Joel's' playing field before levelling out and reaching Earley station. Here a thick forest of beech and oak, extending over hundreds of acres, came up to the railway line and fringed it eastwards for a mile.

My elder sister used often to walk me along a gravelly lane through the woods to the station, passing a favourite, red-brick house with tall gables decorated with ornate barge-boards which stood close to the line. Gates across the lane, protecting the rails, were opened by the signalman, who came down from his signal box to swing them open by hand. His signal box was tall and narrow with small windows and a skimpy roof. It was made of horizontal, overlapping planks, once bright yellow, now faded and muddy, and on its front wall a green enamel sign with white letters read: EARLEY. When I was five, I thought this was the signalman's name and always called him 'Mr Earley' when asking to go into his box.

There were two platforms connected by a concrete footbridge. The Up platform – for London – was nearest the woods; behind it lay a couple of sidings with accommodation for emptying railway petrol tank wagons. The Down platform – for Reading – carried the station office: a substantial, two-storey building with lower walls of brick and upperworks clad in horizontal planking under a hip gable roof.

The station was only 200 yards from a busy main road yet it was smothered in silence and had a magical air of remoteness from the twentieth century. Facing Reading, my back to the footbridge, I would see a tall signal cantilevered out over the tracks, the narrow old signal box and the tracks curving sharply to the right out of sight. From the chimney of the red-brick house woodsmoke, rising blue against the silent, dark green trees, was the only movement. Then the clear 'ting-ting' of a signal box bell would bring the signalman to his levers, his body shadowy within the box. He heaved against the levers, wires squealed over pulleys, the Up line signal arms were raised. Soon an engine of the most antique kind would come into view, leaning to the curve, its tall, thin chimney snorting like a winded horse as it accelerated from the summit of the climb, its exhaust beat uneven – 'dot and carry one' I used to call it – and towing a train of equally ancient green coaches with windowed lookouts for the guard raised above coach roof level. Gasping a rapid staccato, missing every fourth beat, the Victorian engine took its drumming coaches past in a cloud of steam at 30 mph and, followed by my hungry eyes, accelerated up a long straight to a mysterious curve and vanished.

That long, tapering distance and the curve which blotted out the rest of the line was one of the great romances of my five-year-old life – what was it like, just around the corner? Those disappearing rails created in me a lasting curiosity for things just out of sight.

Starting school at St Anne's in Caversham, I rode by bus past the Southern engine shed. The pavement and the tracks were separated only by a railing fence so that engines standing against the buffers were only a few feet from the road. This magnetic attraction was countered each morning by the obligation to go to school – I do not remember ever playing truant, not even for the railway – but on the return home it drew me irresistibly. Each evening, those of us who went home by bus were formed into a crocodile and marched to the bus stop; it did not take me long to find a technique for deserting, missing the bus and thus becoming free to visit the engine shed.

A gate gave access from the pavement to a dozen locomotives; those closest to the road were 'dead', that is, not in steam; those nearest the shed building were being serviced for duty. The men always seemed friendly. I could walk round an engine with its driver while he oiled it, sit in the cab while the fireman stoked his

Earley station, on the edge of hundreds of acres of woodlands, as I remember it from 1944 to 1952. The picture was taken in 1950. The railway's magic was partly due to its hanging back in an earlier era. (Lens of Sutton Collection)

Looking towards Wokingham from the Up main at Earley station in 1930, before electrification. The signal box and its name board date back to South Eastern Railway days – before 1899. (Lens of Sutton Collection)

Earley signal box in 1962 with a smart, Southern Region nameplate. The signalman is Jack Moles. Jack spent his entire railway career at Earley station, starting on the platform as a porter. Jack was a keen gardener and clock repairer – including maintaining the South Eastern Railway pendulum clock in the signal box. He was signalman here from sometime in the 1930s until 1965 when the signalling was automated and taken into the control of Reading 'Panel'. (Author)

The interior of Earley signal box not really any different, in 1962, to when I first went in there in 1944/45. (Author)

fire up to running condition or play drivers on the dead engines by the road. I was taken to see an engine that had been standing so long that it had two birds' nests, one in the V of two spokes of a driving wheel and another in the cab and the men had postponed bringing the engine into service until the birds had flown.

After the engine shed my way home took me thirty feet above the Southern shunting yard, which was in a cutting between the road and the Great Western embankment. It was fun to watch ancient tank engines shunting wagons, rolling them along, changing tracks, free-wheeling, till they came up with a crash against a line of stationary trucks. Then, one memorable evening, I saw a Great Western 'King' class engine come onto the embankment beyond the sidings. I had a wonderful, broadside view of his side-rods swinging easily as he braked for the station, his massive boiler polished green, his copper and brass gleaming, the last word in elegance and strength. I was converted into a 'Western' man immediately.

The Great Western station then became my second home; indeed, in 1947 it was 'home' to a regular crowd of boys who spent all day, in their holidays, watching the working. At the east end of the station, outside a wire fence, on top of an embankment scuffed bare of grass by our shoes, a dead tree gave comfortable seating for several boys and the rest stood or sat by the fence. We were warned of the approach of trains by a tall, wooden signal carrying four arms on three posts, branching like an angular candelabra; and we waited for each express in company with the station's stand-by engine, a 'Saint' or a 'Bulldog' which, between bouts of shunting, rested on a siding almost within arm's reach.

Up express trains, London bound, which were booked to call at Reading, stood for at least five minutes at the platform opposite our perch, giving us broadside views of 'Kings' and 'Castles' at rest and starting away under the cloud of their hugely exciting, noisy exhausts. They began with a crashing beat, four explosions for each turn of their driving wheels —NOW—HERE—WE—GO— a rhythm and a volume suggesting indomitable courage and irresistible power quite unlike any sound that even the best Southern engines made.

Between the Western and Southern stations, below our vantage, was a large timber shack which served as a canteen for Thames Valley bus crews. As soon as an Up train stopped, the fireman would go onto the tender to put the water hose in and fill up the tank while he shovelled coal forward and the driver came through the fence to fill his tea can at the canteen. He did so under the admiring gaze of a dozen boys hoping for a friendly nod and a short 'Hello lad'. Some men responded, others were, I think, disconcerted at this concentration of hero worship. I recall my thrill at seeing close-up his faded blue, soot-smudged overalls – even being *brushed* by them – as he bent and climbed through the strands of wire – this man who drove 'Kings' from Plymouth to Paddington.

One lunchtime the driver of a 'King' which had stopped at Reading on an Up express had gone into the Thames Valley canteen and had not emerged by the time the train's guard had given 'Right Away'. The fireman on the engine was blowing the whistle and us boys were watching the canteen with interest, wondering what had gone wrong.

A drizzly day at Earley station doesn't stop the devoted train spotters – bike leant against railings. An 'S15' class Mixed Traffic 4-6-0, No. 30837, is passing on the Up main. The powerful S15s were introduced in 1927 and were very similar to the N15 'King Arthur' class – the only major difference being that the S15 had a 5-foot 7-inch driving wheel while the N15s had 6-foot 7-inch wheels as befitted a crack express locomotive. (Photographer unknown)

As one wandered about the shed, soaking up the atmosphere, there was sure to be an engine being turned by a friendly shed driver. This is a very powerful 1917-designed 'N' class for goods and passenger work. By the time I was walking round the shed, they had been fitted with smoke deflectors on each side of the smokebox but were otherwise unaltered. This was photographed in August 1931. It became 31816 under BR numbering. (Dr Jack Hollick/Author's Collection)

The canteen door burst open, out came the engine driver – backwards – dragging by the lapels of his jacket a bus man. Both men were rather red in the face. 'Right then, we're outside now,' shouted the engine driver, 'now tell me my "King" isn't as good as the *Mallard*.'* His fireman blew an agonised screech on the whistle – 'Come on, *Come on*' – the driver broke away, up the bank, through the fence past an astonished crowd of boys and, for the benefit of the bus man, made the fastest exit from Reading that I saw for many years.

On the Down main platform at Reading, aged seven, pennies warm and sticky in my hand, I would go to the stand-by engine and ask its driver 'Want a cup of tea, mister?' The driver, good-natured and understanding, would say, 'That's very kind of you, sonny. Yes please.' When I returned with the tea, I had to climb onto the footplate to give the driver the cup and did not dismount until I was told to do so. When the engine went shunting, to remove a horsebox, milk tank or parcels van from the rear of a passenger train, I went too and learned about footplate work from the age of seven on *Saint David*, last of her class, and on *Seagull* and *Skylark*, last of the 'Bulldogs'.

Drivers appreciated people – even small boys – who took an interest in their engine and would explain the working with great patience. It was a fascinating experience. To look through the firehole at the furnace seven or ten feet long; to see the driver pulling up or winding round the big, steel handles to make the engine move; to feel that great mass of metal move smoothly; to hear the long, breathless 'haaah' of the ejector steam from the chimney to release the brakes and the burping, gurgling sound which happened when the brakes were fully released and the ejector was allowed to continue; the juicy 'ffutt' when the throttle, or regulator, was opened before the first barking exhaust beat; the 'spit-spit-spit' of the mechanical vacuum pump, which could be heard when the engine was free-wheeling; and the hissing, sucking 'sheeesh' of inrushing air through the valve when the brakes were applied. When the fireman turned on the water from the tender and then the steam jet to force water through the injector into the boiler, there was first a loud, gurgling roar, subsiding when the jet was adjusted to a sweet, modulating whistle, like birdsong – indeed, I heard some men say that the injectors were 'whistling like a linnet'.

These pleasant, varied sounds with which the engine responded to her driver's commands made her seem like a living creature, warm and breathing. Like the footplatemen, I grew fond of them when they ran well and hated them when they misbehaved.

When the engine left the platform I felt I was leaving a quay, putting out onto a silver river of rails. We would pass through the shadow of the East signal box and stop, a wheeled boat isolated in midstream, waiting for the points to change. From the oiled steel and copper strength of the cab with its core of fire, I looked out over the narrow Southern river that flowed between wide banks of sidings lined with

---

* The *Mallard* was an LNER engine that holds the world record for steam speed – 126 ½ mph.

Reading Southern engine shed was the first engine shed I went into, in 1946 or 1947. The gate into the shed was directly from the pavement. The GWR main line is on the embankment. Because of the necessities of the Second World War, antique engines had to be kept in service – adding to the delights of the railway for me – and many others. This picture of an 1883 vintage South Eastern Railway 'F1' express engine was taken in June 1948. The tender still has the old Company name but the engine has received its British Railway number – adding a '3' to the old '1151'. It was withdrawn from service not long after this was taken. I remember them well – how could one forget such a venerable machine. (Dr Jack Hollick/Author's Collection)

A lovely, gleaming ex-works 'U' class, No. 638 (BR 31638), being prepared for duty in August 1931. Apart from the sheet steel smoke deflectors added later, and the alteration of the number, this scene could be 1948 or 1962. (Dr Jack Hollick/Author's Collection)

This ex-London & South Western '700' class goods engine was photographed on Reading Southern shed in August 1931. D. S. Barrie, GWR Operating Officer and railway historian, is part of the visiting group, his camera case hanging down his left side. These engines were very much part of the scene at Reading in 1948. (Dr Jack Hollick/Author's Collection)

Reading South station, *c.* 1963. It was a nice little station and was additionally enchanting because it was so utterly different to the GWR station just a few yards to the north. Quite different types of steam engines and its very handsome electric trains – nothing as magnificently built and upholstered exists today – and they ran every half an hour to Waterloo. The architecture – signals and signal boxes – as well as the cast iron and bricks and mortar was so *different*. The plain, mid-green paint – just a tiny bit sickly – and the branch line terminus atmosphere. If one was a lover of railways, all aspects of the scene were a matter of delight, if only for the difference. (Author's Collection)

The concourse within Reading South station, *c.* 1960. The chimney of a 'U' class can just be seen. I thought of them as little fat ponies with blinkers back in 1950 – horses were by no means discarded at that time as motive power. The milkman, the coal man and Simmond brewery all used horses, and Simmonds drays were drawn along Broad Street by at least two – if not four – magnificently matched greys. And the silent electric trolleybuses went gliding by. (Author's Collection)

Looking back to the concourse at Reading South. (Author's Collection)

A view showing the close proximity of the Southern and Great Western stations. A 'U' class 2-6-0 prepares to leave for Guildford and Redhill with a couple of cattle trucks in front of the passenger coaches – nice, rural smell for the passengers. August 1932. Over at the GWR a Churchward 'Mogul' 2-6-0 is on the Up main. So us boys could sit by that far fence and enjoy continuous views of steam and engines standing around or moving about. Wooden GWR signals, whose arms went elegantly down and brash Southern signals whose arms waved, slightly hysterically, in the air. (Dr Jack Hollick/Author's Collection)

coaches and wagons, dotted with Victorian and Edwardian locomotives, and saw the silent green serpents of the 'Southern Electric' go gliding up and down the stream.

In between rides on engines, I joined a group of boys and spent hours – a large part of my life in fact – sitting at the west end of the Up main platform. We prided ourselves on being able to recognise any class of engine at a mile in clear weather, each of us wanting to be the first to shout correctly the type that was approaching. 'Elbow steam pipes,' we would yell, 'a Star!' and then jump about and cheer as 4021 *British Monarch* came racing through the station at 70 mph.

At one o'clock each lunchtime any boys on the station would gather on the Up platform, about thirty yards from its western end and wait for the passing of the 8.30 a.m. Plymouth to Paddington express. They chose their stand carefully so as to see the exact moment when the rear coach separated from the main train; they might even see the guard pull the special lever in the coach – for the 'Plymouth' was a slip coach train.

At about 1.5 p.m. the signal on the gantry routing the train to the Up platform was lowered, and if the road was clear right through the station, the special 'slipping distant' signal below the main arm was also lowered; if it remained at 'Caution', the train had to stop to uncouple the coach. The train came free-wheeling around the side of the West box, 'King'-hauled, snaking over the junctions, swerving into the platform line at 20 mph. As soon as the slip coach separated from the main train – the driver always seemed to know exactly when – the big engine erupted into life and went storming away, leaving the slipped coach to run gently by the platform – accompanied by some boys running alongside – and to come to a stand at the head of the subway stairs.

The slip guard stepped down from his compartment in the leading end of the coach as his passengers hurried past and, looking through the guard's open door, we could see the slipping lever pulled to drop the coupling off the hook and the brake handle he used to bring the coach to a stand. As we looked, a tank engine came sneaking up to the coach, the buffers meeting with a 'clonk'. The coupling-up process was always fun to watch and made a fitting end to the show. The engine pushed against the coach, fascinating me with the terrible ease with which it compressed the hidden springs inside the buffers till the circular heads were hard against their stocks. A shunter, crouching between the rails, slung the locomotive's heavy coupling link over the coach draw-hook and shortened its length with a few turns of the screw. Grasping the coaches and the locomotive's vacuum brake pipes, one in each hand, he locked them together with a dextrous twist of his wrists and secured them with a cotter pin.

He scrambled onto the platform, raised an oily hand to the driver. 'Righto, Harry!' The engine then withdrew to its siding to wait for an Up stopping train to which it could attach the coach so that it could return to Paddington for the Down working next day.

By the time I was ten, I was tall enough to ride my mother's bicycle standing up and I began to explore the area around Reading. I discovered a little signal box in Sonning Cutting, close to a bridge which crossed over the line and gave the box its name: Woodley Bridge. After several hours spent sitting on the parapet staring down at the box, I willed the signalman to ask me in.

Harold Summerfield's box had eight levers, two for each track through the cutting, and provided me with a perfect school to learn the basic principles of semaphore signalling. Harold was patient even when I turned up day after day, explaining everything and allowing me to ring the bells and pull the levers.

It was hard work for him, anyway, because traffic was heavy, bells had to be answered quickly and levers pulled over snappily, yet he found time to teach me the art of signalling. Not for twenty years did I realise how much more difficult he made his work for my benefit.

Harold and the various engine drivers were good friends to me; Reading station and its complicated working was perfectly familiar; the whole range of railway operations was my hobby and filled all my out-of-school life.

Then, in 1952, my father became so ill that he was obliged to sell his small shop and go into the country. He had always wanted to live on the Berkshire Downs and managed to buy a run-down cottage in Childrey, four miles from White Horse Hill, which pleased him mightily but appalled me. I felt that no railway station in the world could be as busy and exciting as Reading, least of all some sleepy little place far out in the Berkshire vale.

In recognition of my devotion to railways, I was allowed to travel by myself, by train, to the village station, Challow, while the rest of the family led the removal van in the Austin Seven. I caught the 2.40 p.m. Down stopper from my magnificent Reading station, convinced that my life was ruined, and headed westwards with a sinking heart.

Woodley Bridge signal box, where my signalman's education began in 1951. A floor 10 feet long by 8 feet front to back housing a distant and home signal lever for each track, four block bells, four block instruments, and a hand-coloured diagram of the tracks. The signals are, typically, 'off' for both the Up main and Up relief lines. They could also be cleared for both of the Down lines. Approximately 120 trains passed here in an 8-hour shift. A 'Castle' is coming by with – probably – the 11.45 Bristol. *c.* 1957. (Peter Barlow/Author's Collection)

The box was open for the Early and Late turns, switched out on nights. Various men worked it. The young men who were there most often and allowed me into their box were Fred Hodrien, Harold Summerfield and Ron Warner. I suppose I improved as I learned but it was always very kind of them to let me into a very cramped space, make me tea, stand over me and instruct me when it would have been much easier for them just to get on and do the job themselves. The edge of the signal box frames the left of the picture, the wonderful engine coming through is a 'County' class 4-6-0. There is a spare firing shovel sticking up on the tender. There was always the possibility of the fireman accidentally throwing the shovel into the fire. (Peter Barlow/Author's Collection)

Woodley Bridge with 3217 passing on the Up relief line hauling a parcels train for Paddington. The vehicle behind the engine is an ex-LNER parcels van. The fourth van is an LMS job. (Peter Barlow/Author's Collection)

Shottesbrooke box, 4 ⅜ miles east of Woodley Bridge box, was identical in every respect to Woodley Bridge. From this view one can appreciate the good nature of the Woodley Bridge signalmen in letting me into their very cramped space. (Peter Barlow/Author's Collection)

Chapter Two

A Station in the Vale

'Challer! Challer!' a Berkshire voice called as the 2.40 from Reading squealed to a halt for the eighth time since starting its journey. A tall porter in a dark-blue uniform and peaked cap, his red tie blowing in the wind, passed the narrow window of my compartment, calling 'Challer' energetically as if he enjoyed mispronouncing the station's name. I lowered the window by its leather strap, turned the outside handle and stepped down onto the platform.

The porter was collecting tickets and turned back for mine, took it and closed my door firmly. 'All right?' shouted the guard from five coaches back. 'Right you be,' replied the porter. The guard blew his pea-whistle and waved his green flag above his head at the same time. There was an answering 'toot' from the 'Hall' at the head of the train before she went snuffing gently away from the station.

I watched it pass a fair-sized signal box and turn across points from Down relief to Down main line. The driver then put on steam and with an accelerating rhythm the train drove west for Swindon, the continuous, snorting exhaust beat growing faint and broken as the breeze took the noise where it pleased till a curve in the track shut off sight and sound. A signal at the platform's end thudded up to 'Danger' and I turned to go, getting a look of friendly curiosity and a nodded Berkshire 'Mornin'' from the porter as I did so.

I walked up a wide, gravel slope to the main road, which crossed the railway on a bridge, and looked around. The railway came from the Reading direction four tracks wide in a shallow cutting through gently undulating fields, under the bridge, between the platforms, merging into double track just beyond the signal box. The box was on the down-side of the line, the cutting not quite reaching the level of its window sills. The station office was on the up-side and looked modern; a plain red-brick building, long and low. Beyond it was an open space taken up by a car park and some allotments, on the far side of which was a row of terraced, slate-fronted cottages for station staff. At the left-hand end of the row was a detached house that looked as if it belonged to the station master and at the other end was a public house, the Prince of Wales. The road ran north and fell downhill, out of sight between the pub and a fine old farmhouse. Beyond the terrace there was only the grey sky and, very faint, the horizon of a line of hills upon which stood a very prominent clump of trees.

Looking south, the road dropped off the bridge, past the junction with a lane lined on both sides with tall elm trees, rose and disappeared over swelling ground, the ridge lined with evenly spaced trees. A solitary, black car came over the brow and ran down the slope towards me. Two or three houses showed and in the far distance I could see the long, clean, clear outline of the Berkshire Downs. My town-dull ears began to register country sounds – I heard the wind hissing in the roadside grass and high overhead a bird I guessed to be a skylark sang as if it had some serious obligation to do so. 'This is a queer place for a railway station,' I thought, as the wind began to feel chill, and, following the instructions I had been given before I left Reading, went down to the lane. 'Childrey 2 ½' said the signpost and, hoping I would get a lift, I set off.

The lane made a series of S-bends before straightening past a mock-Tudor farmhouse, on, between tall, ragged hedges past a derelict brickworks, mysterious and interesting and over the marshy remains of a canal. I stopped to rest and a moorhen dashed for cover. Beyond the canal the road ran through clean fields bordered by well-kept hedges, rose past an expensive-looking stable and came to a T-junction where a sign pointed left for Childrey.

I walked past an old orchard screening an ancient manor house and, rounding a sharp bend, found myself in the main street of the village. 'Go to the far end of the street, we're next to the Crown,' my father had said. I passed an ivy-grown farm by a pond, a row of thatched cottages, between two rows of brick cottages and saw the road rising steeply out of the village in a deep cutting arched in by tall beeches – there was the Crown and on a high bank above the road was a long, thatched cottage – my new home.

The sound of express trains as they whistled through Challow came up clearly to the village – especially in the quiet of Sunday. Each time I heard that faint, clear note and the drumming rhythm of the wheels, sounding curiously hollow with distance, I longed to be at the lineside. As soon as we had settled in and my services as a general assistant were no longer required, I took myself off to the station.

After a couple of long days spent sitting on a four-wheel barrow, being nodded at by the station master and ignored by a very stern-looking porter, I met the tall man who had taken my ticket the day I had arrived from Reading.

'Hi-up then,' he said, 'I shall want that barrow,' and sat down on it with me. 'D'you live around here then? I haven't seen you before.'

'You saw me a couple of weeks ago when I got off the train here from Reading. We've just moved to Childrey.'

'They told me you liked trains, because you've been here a lot in the last couple of days.'

'I love the engines. I used to ride on the Pilot at Reading and there was a signal box in Sonning Cutting I used to visit almost every evening after school – do you think I could get into the signal box here?'

'Well, of course. Ken Rowlands is on now. Haven't you met him? He lives in Childrey. Come on, I'll take you up. What's your name, mine's Sam – Sam Loder.'

Sam went before me up the stairs of the box and I heard him saying, 'Hi-up, Ken. I've got a young lad here from Childrey wants to see the box.'

The splendid electric buses came silently and without smelly fumes to the stations. Just out of shot, to the right of the busmen there was a stall, pushed back against the wall of the Bay platforms where a man sold mugs of tea, cakes, buns and sandwiches. A 'thruppeny bit' (1 ½ p) was sufficient for a platform ticket and a mug of tea in 1950. (Author's Collection)

No. 4903 *Astley Hall* stands in the special siding reserved for the Reading Station Pilot. It was on engines standing on and working out of that siding that I first gained access to the footplate, aged six, in 1947. Sitting on the Pilot here and being taken around the station when the engine was called out for shunting passenger stock, I learned a lot about how to work an engine – and about how the men conducted themselves when carrying out their duties. When I was twelve and a driver asked me if I would like to drive, I had a very sound theoretical knowledge of how to go on and also of the way to behave when moving an engine about on the tracks. This picture is of rather later date, around 1964, than when I rode on *Seagull*, *Skylark* and *Saint David* but I'm glad to be able to include it. On the left is the Thames Valley bus drivers' canteen and the Southern station behind that, just out of view. (Rod Blencowe Archive)

Looking across to the Up main, No. 5 platform, from the Down main, No. 4 platform. No. 4903 is now standing on the Down relief middle line with a van. No spotters in sight, this must have been taken on a school day. (Rod Blencowe Archive)

Locospotters sitting along the edge of No. 5 platform at Reading. The siding to the right of the incoming 'Hall' was where the Station Pilot engine used to stand awaiting the arrival of the slip coach off the 8.30 a.m. Plymouth at 12.50 p.m. When the coach had been brought to a stand by its guard, right opposite the stairway down to the subway, the engine would come out onto the platform line, collect the coach and later attach it to the back of a London-bound 'all stations' passenger train. Over on the left a 'King Arthur' class No. 30783 *Sir Balin* has brought into No. 3 platform a train from Portsmouth and is now waiting to reverse out of the Bay to Reading GW shed. On Bay 2 is a 'Hall' awaiting the 'off' with a Newbury line stopping train. (Johnathan Ashman/Courtesy Mike Esau)

The view west from platform 2 of the Down bays at Reading, *c.* 1958. On the right, 76016 is waiting to leave with a Portsmouth train, and a GWR engine is on the left. A 'Hall' has just joined the main line for Paddington from the Berks & Hants Line with a train from Plymouth if not further west than that. On the signal gantry the signal is lowered for a train to turn off the Down main to the Berks & Hants line. These were the heavenly delights awaiting anyone with one penny to spend on a platform ticket at Reading – ten platforms for one penny. (Courtesy Les Reason/Author's Collection)

No. 70026, the engine that went down the bank at Milton in 1955, comes roaring through Reading, blowing off steam with twelve coaches behind the tender on the 7.30 a.m. Carmarthen–Paddington 'Red Dragon' express. Much to the disappointment of the gallery of boys, the driver is not blowing his howling 'chime' whistle. (Courtesy Les Reason/Author's Collection)

'From Childrey?' said a puzzled voice. 'Who can that be?' I stepped from the stairs below Sam to the operating room floor. Ken Rowlands was a slim, fair-haired man with blue eyes and a quiet, gentle manner. I introduced myself, 'We've just moved in,' I finished, realising I would be saying those words quite a lot in the next few weeks. He smiled, extended his hand and said, 'I've heard about the new arrivals. Pleased to meet you.'

Practically, my only experience of signal boxes up to that moment had been of the tiny, cramped Woodley Bridge box. Challow was quite the opposite and quite superb. It must have been 40 feet long and 10 feet wide,* its polished linoleum floor reflecting any of the fifty-one levers that happened to be pulled over. I recognised the yellow lever at each end of the row as operating the distant signals, the red levers as working stop signals and the black/white levers that placed an audible danger signal – a 'shot' or detonator – on the rail for emergencies. There were also black levers, blue levers, blue/brown and red/yellow levers that I had not seen before; all of them had polished brass plates giving details of their function. There were a lot of instruments and telephones and, though the box handled only half the traffic that passed Woodley Bridge, its work was much more interesting and important.

The signalman spent a lot of his time sending and receiving information over the telephones concerning train running, making and answering enquiries to and from other boxes, which resulted in goods trains leaving Challow's Down relief line for the Down main or switching from the Up main to the Up relief line just as he thought would be best for the free running of the express trains. I felt completely overwhelmed by the complexity of it all and went home at teatime, my head full of bell codes, trying to understand it all. I remember telling my mother that the man who could operate Challow box must be a species of genius.

Challow box became an irresistible attraction and the following afternoon I was knocking on the box door asking to be let in. Ken never refused, though I am sure there were times when he would have liked to be on his own. I saw from the lever brasses that the black levers worked points, the blue levers operated bolts to hold certain points firmly in position while a train was passing over them, the blue/brown levers were for electrically operated points and the red/yellow levers worked simultaneously the distant and home signals of something called 'Circourt IBS'.

Ken explained that the points from the Up platform to Up main and from the Down main to Down platform line were considered to be too far away to be worked by a lever and rodding so they were 'motor worked' instead. The relevant lever was pulled over two thirds of its travel and then the handle of the hand-generator, which he called the 'hurdy-gurdy', was turned to make a current to turn the motor at the points. An indicator showed when the points had been correctly set and then the lever could be dropped to its final position and the necessary signals lowered for the route. The IBS – Intermediate Block Section – had been installed only a few weeks before I arrived and replaced a signal box similar to Woodley Bridge, called 'Circourt' after a nearby farm. Instead of a signalman lowering semaphore signals from a 'break-section' box, colour light distant and stop

---

* The actual dimensions were 25 feet by 11 feet.

signals had been installed, those on the Up main and Up relief lines being worked from Challow by levers 6 and 10 respectively, while Wantage Road, the next box eastwards, worked those on the Down lines. Because the blue/brown and red/yellow levers were no more than switches in an electric circuit, they had only short, steel handles so that the signalman would not forget himself and pull them over with a mighty swing.

There were three 'block bells' in the box paired to three 'block indicators'. One pair signalled trains over the Up and Down main lines to Uffington, the next box westwards, the others were for the Up and Down relief and Up and Down main lines to Wantage Road. No train could come towards Challow from either Uffington or Wantage Road until the signalman at Challow had given his permission by acknowledging a bell code and by turning the block indicator to 'Line Clear'. No train could pass Challow in either direction until the signalman at Uffington or Wantage Road had given his permission; the action of turning the block indicator to 'Line Clear' actually released an electric lock on the stop signal, giving access to the next man's section of line.

Trains were signalled along the track by a series of bell codes – asking permission for the train to proceed, warning of its imminent approach and saying when it had passed and the section was clear for the next train. It was just a routine and simple enough once you got the hang of it; with my experience at Woodley Bridge to draw upon, I was able to grasp Challow's *routine* quickly but the *regulation* of goods and passenger traffic required a far wider experience, a full knowledge of the train service throughout the twenty-four hours of a day, an understanding of the layouts at other signal boxes and the running times of all the various types of trains between point A and point B. This would take months to pick up.

I worked the bells and levers under Ken's directions all week. There was a special pleasure in setting the route from Up main to Up relief line and seeing a goods or stopping passenger train turning into the slow line at my direction. There was an even greater pleasure to be gained in lowering the signals on the Down relief line, hearing the engine of a goods train whistle acknowledgement and actually start up in response to my signal. But there was one train each afternoon that Ken would not let me signal, the Up Bristolian; when the bell rang for it at about five past five, he would say, 'Let me see to that.'

This train was 'King'-hauled and, with seven coaches, had to cover the 117 ½ miles from Bristol to Paddington in 105 minutes, an average start to stop speed of 67 ½ mph. It was the fastest train in Britain – possibly in the world. The service had been introduced by the Great Western Railway in 1935 to mark the centenary of the company, had been withdrawn in 1939 and now, in June 1954, had been reintroduced. With a massive 'King' hauling a piffling load, some very fast running had been achieved with times well within the official schedule, the train had taken on the prestige of the pre-war Cheltenham Flyer and become utterly sacred. Hence Ken's concern that it should not be accidentally delayed at Challow by a schoolboy.

Imagine my delight when, on Friday evening, after five afternoons of practice, he trusted me sufficiently to 'pull off' for this Train of Trains! I cannot remember enjoying any train so much as that one. I had not only signalled the finest train in the country, I had been recognised as trustworthy by the signalman who had to 'take the can back' if I did anything stupid. My confidence soared as I leant professionally from the window to observe the train as it thundered past at 90 mph behind 6015 *King Richard III*. I actually left the box early that night and tore home, bursting indoors to tell my parents, 'Ken let me pull off for the Bristolian this evening!'

Before I left that evening, Ken had said, 'I'm on nights next week but Bill Mattingley will be here on late turn, I've had a word with him and it'll be all right for you to come up when he's on. I dare say he'd be glad of some help with the box – he does barbering here on Thursdays.'

The following Monday I went along to the box at teatime and met Bill. He already had an assistant and was lying in his armchair, his legs stretched out along a low bench, enjoying a conversation with a colleague called 'Wally' or 'Wal', whom I gathered worked at Wantage Road box. Bill got out of his chair as I came in, roared 'Here he is!', crushed my hand, fell back into his chair and roared again, 'Well – how's the boy doing?' Bill was a big man with a strong voice, a loud laugh and a presence that filled the box.

Lying in a chair, holding a telephone, Bill waved his free arm in the direction of his assistant. 'That there's Basil, my mate. He lives over in the station houses; his Dad's the lampy (lampman), and he comes over most evenings to help with the frame – especially Thursday nights. Eh, Bas?' Basil, with fully two years more than my thirteen, grinned at Bill and agreed but did little more than nod at me – we were immediately jealous of each other, I think – but Bill did not appear to notice, only returned to his interrupted conversation with Wally at Wantage. 'Yes then, Wal ...' A bell rang and Basil moved confidently to answer it, one of the several telephones rang, Basil knew which one and handed it to the recumbent Bill – he even switched goods trains in and out of the relief lines without asking! There was nothing for me to do and I felt thoroughly squashed but stuck it out until 'going home time' at ten.

The following evening Bill had two chess wallets on the table, one for a game he was playing with his mate Alec at Steventon, the other for 'Chalky' White, the local policeman, who would come into the box most evenings when Bill was on duty to make his move and have a cup of tea before reporting by public phone to his sergeant at Wantage. Basil and his young brother Robin and I arrived at seven o'clock, 'Chalky' turned up at eight, Bill had tea, milk and sugar for all of us, and we had an interesting party for an hour as Bill, Basil and 'Chalky' argued about chess, Robin tried to do his homework and I had the fifty-one levers all to myself.

I missed only Thursday and Friday evening that week and on Saturday had the box to myself.

'Come in! How's the boy?' boomed Bill. 'Need your help; ol' Basil's gone to the cricket over Frilford. I missed you on Thursday, had to manage the box and do the barbering too. I expected one of you and neither turned up. I'll tell you what, you promise to be here, for certain sure, Thursday evenings and I can guarantee you the box to work. There's only two or three customers, so I shan't keep you long.'

I replied that it did not matter if he kept me all night and we sealed the bargain over a cup of his tea.

A few minutes later Sam Loder came to the box carrying a shotgun and a wireless. Bill poured him the dregs of the pot, Sam took a cushion and sat in comfort on the back window sill, looking over the fields and a line of trees, shotgun at the ready, tea within reach, and John Arlott droning out a cricket commentary – a comforting accompaniment to a quiet afternoon.

'What do you think of our new station master then, Sam?' asked Bill.

'Fred Halford? Not a bad sort of chap, bit quiet. He comes from somewhere up Worcester way, don't he – the Bromyard branch, Basil said.'

'Suckley, Mr Halford told me, p'r'aps that is the Bromyard line. He was a station master there for a few years but he's been a signalman since before the war. Did you know that him and his wife worked the same box together, turn and turn about, during the war?'

'Get away!' exclaimed Sam. 'That must have been awkward for getting meals; they'd hardly have seen each other. I wonder if they had to do a night shift.'

'He never said, but that's just the sort of thing you would think of, Loder,' Bill said with mock severity.

'How's your strapper getting on then?' said Sam, changing the subject.

'Oh, he'll do, he might come to work here one day and then he'll find a difference – no coming and going as he pleases, just eight hours a day seven days a week.'

'Oh-ho!' cheered Sam. 'You don't do so bad, sitting on your backside with plenty of help.'

'Depends what else you want to do,' said Bill. 'I've got my bees to see to – I lost a swarm back in May because I was here on early turn, now that hive'll be producing nothing for me this summer.'

I had never heard anything as near a complaint as this before, neither had it occurred to me that railwaymen might have some other interests besides their work, probably because I only spoke to them about railways. I wondered if I *would* be so keen if I came to work in the box day after day.

'Don't you like your job here, then, Bill?' I asked.

'Yes, o'course I do,' he replied, 'I'm my own boss more'n if I worked in a shop or a factory, but it gets in the way sometimes.'

'Go on!' Sam said, exasperated. 'If you was in a shop all day, you'd never get a chance to see to your bees, shift work's ideal for you if you're bee-keeping on the side.'

'Yes, I know, you're right. Challow's a good steady old number wi' some railway work to do –'

Sam broke in, 'And plenty of people to help you do it – hey up! Here comes Mr Halford.'

My heart leaped and sank like a stone – the Station Master!

'Do you think he'll mind?' I asked. Bill looked at Sam, Sam looked back at him and hid his shotgun behind a locker.

'I dunno. What's he coming over for anyway on his day off?'

The door opened and Mr Halford came up the stairs. Bill got up, Sam was already standing by the wall, I was trying to hide behind the row of levers.

'Afternoon, sir,' said Bill nervously, 'very fine day, everything all right?'

'Yes thanks, I was just out for a stroll – who's this?' he pointed towards me.

'That's Adrian, Bill's strapper,' said Sam, quickly, while Bill was groping for words, cheerfully aggressive, 'he's teaching him the job against the day when he comes to work here.'

Bill shot Sam an appealing glance – ('Shut your great mouth!') – and grinned more nervously than ever at the station master.

'Are you learning anything?' he asked me.

'Um … well …'

'When can you give "Line Clear" for a train?'

'When the line is clear for a quarter of a mile ahead of the home signal and all points within that distance are set for the safety of the approaching train.'

'Oh ho! This isn't your first visit. You've done a good job, Bill,' he said with a smile, 'well done.'

Mr Halford was about fifty years old, slightly less than average height, of slim, even slight build with dark hair, going silver, and blue eyes; beside the broad Bill Mattingley and tall Sam Loder, he looked almost frail. He was obviously disposed to be friendly. 'Er … um, we were wondering where Suckley was,' said Bill.

'On the Bromyard branch. It turned off the Worcester to Hereford line near Worcester at Bransford Road Junction and went twenty-seven miles across to Leominster on the Newport to Shrewsbury line. It was a quiet little place, a single track with the boxes open from seven in the morning to half past eight at night – quite a contrast to this place.'

'Did you always work on that line?'

'No, I started at Long Marston in 1928 and worked at various places after that between Blockley and Pershore till I got a class six signalman's job at Fencote on the Bromyard in 1937. Promotion was waiting for dead men's shoes in those days.'

'I went in the RAF before the war,' volunteered Bill, 'and did all right. I'm the strapper round here. I didn't start till 1947. Would you like some tea, Mr Halford?'

'If there's one going.'

'Things were bad in the '30s,' continued Sam, 'I went on the farm when I left school in 1927. Joined the Guards to get away from cowshit and landed up to my neck in bullshit!'

We all laughed, though I thought Mr Halford did so with a slight wince.

'What regiment, Sam?' he asked.

'The Grenadiers,' he said with hint of pride showing through his casual tone. I saw him better then – no wonder he walked so straight and tall. 'I came out in 1933, after three years, went on the Reserve and worked with the branch gang at Faringdon. When the war came I went back to the Colours and my wife joined up too – she came on here as a porter.'

'Ha! That's good,' said Mr Halford, 'my wife worked on the railway too, during the war. We worked Fencote together.' He finished off his tea and put down the cup. 'Ah! That's better, thanks for the tea, Bill. I'll love you and leave you now – keep on with the rules young man.' And he went down the stairs.

When the door had been closed, Sam settled himself back onto the window sill. 'There you are, he's a good bloke – I told you so.'

'Yes, he's all right,' agreed Bill, 'he's been through the mill.'

Chapter Three

On the Fly

After the station master had given his unspoken approval to my presence in the box, I felt secure and visited Ken and Bill frequently. I had to divide my spare time between the box and a part-time job looking after two horses, but I fitted it all in – particularly my promise to Bill – and became quite a good horseman as I learned more about signal box work.

On Thursdays I rushed to get to the signal box so as to have as long as possible 'in charge' without fear of having to share it with Basil. Bill would be loud and hearty in his greetings. 'Well done, young man. Here's the duster, pull off on the Down main for the 4.55.' I would heave over levers 62, 61, 60, 54 and 63, in that order, and feel very confident and proud. Almost all passenger trains on the Down line at Challow originated from Paddington so that signalmen referred to them simply as 'the 8.45' or '4.55' (from Paddington) while Up line expresses were known by their place of origin – the 'Kingswear' or the 'Pembroke' as they were trains *from* those places to Paddington.

In 1954 the 4.55 was followed by the 5.5 and the 2.18 (6.4 Didcot) stopper, which did not stop at Challow, and the 5.14 express, which did, turning into the platform from the Down main through power points 45, signals 62 and 59 being lowered to allow it access to the station. The train rejoined the main line through points 30, bolted by lever 31, signalled by 56, 55 and 54. The levers at Challow were numbered 1 to 63 from left to right – there were eleven spaces. The box faced north so lever 1 was at the west end operating the Up distant signal and lever 63 was at the east end for the Down distant, the levers' position in the frame corresponding with their signals' and points' sequence over the ground.

I asked Bill if No. 1 was always the Up distant.

'No, it could be the Down distant but it is always at the left-hand end of the frame. You want to pop up to Wally's place at Wantage Road, then you'd understand.'

After the 5.55 – the Red Dragon – had passed at about 7 p.m., Bill's customers started to arrive. I walked about the bells and levers, seeing Bill with his spectacles on, poring over some grizzled old neck busy with his clippers – then I felt I was 'on my own'. It was a wonderful feeling.

The express trains and stoppers I knew how to handle, but I had to ask him what to do with the freights.

'There's a 3-2 off Uffington, Bill.'*

'What time is it?' he mumbled, with a comb in his mouth.

'7.28.'

'Let it run!' and I pulled off up the main – 2, 3, 5, 6 and 1 in that order.

The following Monday I was standing with my mother on the green at Childrey, outside Bradbrook's thatched shop, waiting for some people to come out to give us space to get in, when Ken Rowlands came out of a lane by the shop. I introduced him to my mother.

'I do hope he isn't a nuisance to you, Mr Rowlands,' she said, 'he spends a lot of time at the signal box.'

'Oh, not at all,' said Ken, with what might have been a wan smile, 'he's very keen – I don't think you've seen the Fly yet, have you Adrian?'

'The Fly? What's that?'

'The local goods. It comes quite early in the morning to shunt the yard. There's two or three boys from here that go down to ride round the station on it, you've missed it today but if you get down to the station for eight on Wednesday you'll be in time.'

On Wednesday I cycled down to the station with two boys, Peter and Mike. They told me they went down only for the ride on the engine. 'Watching trains all day is silly,' they said. As we cycled along the final stretch of lane before the main road, we could see the steam and hear the noise of a shunting engine at work. We pedalled as fast as we could, up the slope of the bridge, down the station approach, threw our bikes roughly on the ground and dashed onto the platform. 'Who's driving?' panted one boy to the other. 'Can't see ... it's Wilf! Come on, we'll be all right with him,' and they dashed over the footbridge to the upside where the train was shunting.

The engine was one I had never seen before, except in photographs – an 0-6-2 tank No. 5639. According to books, they were confined to South Wales, so I was pleased to see such a rarity. It came into the platform, preparing for a shunt, and Mike asked, 'Can we come up, Wilf, please?'

'You can if you like,' he said, moving his bulk to clear the gangway. Three boys were onto the footplate in three jumps, cramming themselves in till the cab bulged with boys; the fireman was only sixteen.

Sam Loder was in charge of shunting, and it occurred to me that I could go up to Wantage Road to see Wally and his signal box on the Fly if Sam would ask the driver on my behalf, so I waited for an opportunity to speak to him. The engine stopped sharply to shunt a wagon off, placing Sam – leaning on his pole watching the truck bowling along the siding – just below the gangway. I climbed down to the track.

'Hello Sam.'

'Well, I'm blowed! Where have you sprung from?'

---

* See Appendices 1 and 2.

'I've been on the engine. Sam, would you ask the driver if he'd take me to Wantage Road?'

'Wilf's all right. You can ask him yourself, but make sure the others don't hear or he'll say no.' I got back onto the engine feeling nervous about asking the driver a favour when I did not know him.

Wilf brought his tank engine gently into the platform with the whole train in tow. Shunting was over for the day. 'Right then, boys,' said he briskly, 'that's all for now. See you again on Friday.' We shuffled off the engine onto the platform. I felt uneasy at the thought of asking and ashamed of feeling scared. Peter and Mike were heading for the footbridge steps so as to be directly over the engine's funnel when it started off and I was about to follow when Sam, standing a little way off, caught my eye, urging me to ask.

'Er, um ... thank you for the ride, er, Mister,' I said desperately.

'That's all right, son,' replied Wilf, wiping his hands on some cotton waste as he leant over the cab side and grinned down at me.

'Um, I often go into the signal box here and the signalman said I ought to go to see the box at Wantage – er, do you think I could ride up with you?'

Wilf was grinning again, but not down at me. I turned to find Sam standing right behind me, nodding his head vigorously at the driver!

'All right then, jump on at the top end of the platform.'

The tank engine, which was running bunker first, pulled gently through the station toward the Up relief line starting signal – No. 8 lever in the box – which was at 'Danger'. Wilf blew his whistle and I jumped aboard as No. 8 lowered. Half a mile up the line I saw No. 9 arm drop, the IBS colour light distant signal below the arm remaining at amber 'Caution' for a few seconds before changing to green in response to lever 10 being thrown over in the signal box. Wilf looked back along his train until it was safely under way, waved acknowledgement to his guard's 'All Right' wave and then turned to watch the road ahead.

'I'm Wilf and that's my son Steve. What's your name?'

I told him.

'Been on an engine before?'

'Only round Reading station on the Pilot, never on a long journey.'

'Ha! I wouldn't call it long – only three miles.'

'Well, it's all through fields. It looks different when you see it from the engine instead of from a coach.'

'When do you leave school, Adrian?'

'In three years.'

'Steve's been left a year now. You could be doing his job in four years' time – that's not long.' It seemed like a lifetime to me, and I looked admiringly at Steve who could ride around on a steam engine with his dad. A loud bell rang out from above a green box fixed to the side of the cab.

'The Pilot at Reading had one of those. What is it for?'

'That's the ATC. It's a Great Western idea and all our engines are fitted with them. None of the other lines has anything like it. We've just passed Circourt's distant signal at 'All Right' and got the bell but if the signal had been at 'Caution' we'd have got a siren and the brakes would have gone on. You'll see what I mean in a few minutes.'

We rattled merrily through the fields, our white exhaust swirling round twenty assorted wagons which bobbed up and down over the rail joints. 'Look here now,' commanded Wilf. I moved to his side of the cab. 'Look – between the rails ahead – there's a long, thin ramp and a bit further on is the distant signal. We're going over the ramp now.' *Veeeeee* – a siren sounded in the green box. 'Look at the vacuum gauge.' One of the needles was dropping and I could feel the brakes going on. Wilf flicked a switch on the side of the box, the wailing stopped and the needle rose.

'If I hadn't turned it off the brakes would have gone on harder and harder until the train was stopped – even if the regulator was fully open. The ATC tells you when you are approaching a distant signal, it gives you the correct "All Right" or "Caution" signal and would bring you to a stand if you ignored the siren. Once you've acknowledged the "Caution" by turning the thing off, it's up to you to take over the braking and be ready to stop at the first stop signal. It makes life safer when the fog is thick.'

'But what if you turned off the siren and then didn't do any braking yourself?' I asked.

'You'd be a bloody fool,' he said.

He began to brake the train and we ran quietly into the platform at Wantage Road. I got off the engine and thanked Wilf for a lovely ride and an interesting talk. 'You're very welcome,' he said. 'It's nice to see you enjoying yourself.' I turned away as a porter, the image of the stern man I had seen at Challow on several occasions, came across the 'barrow crossing' and up the platform ramp, his shunting pole in his hand. I was so busy wondering whether it was the same man or his identical twin that his slight nod of recognition did not register with me at first – then it sank in and I realised that, somehow, he must work at both stations.

The train drew away preparatory to reversing into the goods yard and I saw, standing on the opposite platform, under an awning, an odd little tank engine, painted bright green with a very tall, thin, black chimney, a small dome of unusual and elaborate shape, a huge, square cab and four tiny driving wheels. I was gripped with excitement – an engine I had never heard of or seen in a picture. I stared in amazement across the tracks and saw that she carried a name – *Shannon* – and on her cab were yellow letters – W.T. Co. No. 5.

Wantage Road box was, from the outside, the twin of Challow. I went in and was greeted by Wally Randall, who had obviously been briefed by Bill to expect me. The box interior also looked exactly like Challow, controlling the same layout with levers numbered 1 to 63.

'So you're Bill's strapper. Pleased to meet you,' he said with a wide smile and a Londonish accent, unusual in our part of the world. He was short and inclined to be stocky, his grey hair brushed straight back from his forehead, his face pale, tending to be fleshy and round and just beginning to become lined. He wore his uniform, blue serge trousers and an open-necked white shirt.

'Everyone says I'm a strapper – what does it mean?'

'Well, I'd have thought that was obvious – a learner.'

'I suppose what I mean is what does a strapper have to do with being a learner – what's the connection?'

'Goodness only knows. It's the word we've used for as long as I've been around. I was a strapper thirty years ago.'

'The engine on the platform is lovely – where does *that* come from?'

'Well, I'd have thought you'd have known that too – answer that bell, it'll be the Weston – that's *Shannon* that used to work the tramway that ran from here to the town. I only knew it when they were hauling goods. We used to get old *Shannon* out on the main line to do shunting now and then, but back in the '20s the tram took passengers too. They say that all the station staff here were allowed free travel and the landlord and his wife at the Rifle Volunteer just up the road, too. If you come to the window – look, see that siding curving down the middle of the station yard, you can see it's heading out to the main road; that was the start of the line to Wantage till they put the blocks up in 1945. It went right past the pub's front door. I s'pose that's why they had free travel, to make up for the inconvenience.'

'The engine looks very old.'

'Didn't you see the plaque? It tells you there that she was built in 1857. When the line was closed, the Great Western did her up and put her on show – very nice of them really. You wouldn't get no modern firm thinking of a thing like that. Answer that "Approach", get the road from Lockinge and pull off up the main.'

I looked at the instruments and rang the bell marked 'Lockinge' – four beats. Back came the code as the indicator needle swung to 'Line Clear'. I walked to the end of the box to pull off 2, 3, 5, 6 and 1.

'What are you doing?' asked Wally.

'Pulling off up the main.'

'Aha! You're not at Challow now. Up the main is 62, 61, 60, 54 and 63,' Wally beamed triumphantly. I pulled the levers over feeling decidedly awkward – these were the Down main levers at Challow! 'You see,' said Wal, 'the box here faces south, opposite to Challow, so when the levers are numbered from left to right, 1 to 63, 1 is at the opposite end of the box to Challow's 1.' I saw the point and felt sheepish about it, but it was still awkward to be pulling Down line levers for an Up line train!

'There's another thing you could explain, Wally. The porter on the station this morning, I've seen him at Challow a lot, how does he work here too?'

'That's Harry Strong. He's a reliefman and covers all over the Swindon district though they keep him up this end – Challow to Steventon.'

'As far away as that!' I exclaimed.

'Huh! He considers himself lucky. They could send him to Ludgershall every day.'

I didn't know where that was, but it sounded like a long way away. 'He doesn't say much,' I ventured.

'Harry's all right, the very best. Him and Albert Stanley are about the oldest hands on this patch; they've both been on since about 1920. Harry was a signalman at Circourt and went portering on the relief when they took the box away – there's not much he can't do. He made 'em all sit up and take notice a few years back when he was at Circourt. It was all over the slip coach on the Up Weston in the morning. Slip coaches were taken off in 1939 as an economy measure for the war and were reintroduced in 1946 so the blokes had got rusty about recognising the different tail lamps – I wouldn't be so bold as to say I wouldn't have made the same mistake. You've seen the Weston going up with the slip tail lamp on red and white side by side – haven't you? When that coach comes off at Didcot the main train goes on with the special tail lamp – red over red – to show the slip's gone, so if you ever see that train showing that lamp at Challow you'll know he's lost his slip coach somewhere.

'Well, on this occasion, the slip guard pulled his lever just after Knighton Crossing – no one ever heard how he came to do it – and then, instead of letting the coach roll to Uffington, he put the brakes on there and then and stopped out in the section. The chap at Uffington saw the double tail lamps, thought it was the slip lamp, gave "Train out of Section" to Knighton and the "Line Clear" for the Up stopper. The guard was slow in getting down onto the track and didn't go back to protect the coach with "shots". Luckily for him the "packers" were working a bit towards Knighton, saw the coach stopped, heard the stopper coming fast, put two and two together and got some detonators down on the rail. The stopper pulled up about a hundred yards from the slip.

'In the meantime, the train had passed Challow and the bloke *there* didn't notice anything wrong and sent the "Train out" to Uffington. It was Harry at Circourt who spotted that the slip was missing and sent me the 5-5, "Train Divided". Thanks to the gang, there was no harm done, except to several blokes' pride – they all had to go to Bristol for it.'

I soaked all this up, trying to grasp the casual mention of the operation of so many rules – the gang's actions, Harry's, what the guard ought to have done – Wally spoke with such familiarity about things which seemed so complicated and even mysterious. I burned to know more.

'But what if a train slips a carriage at Swindon according to schedule? It will come up through here with the "slip gone" signal showing. How would you know whether it was *meant* to be showing or whether it was a mistake like the one you've just told me about?'

'Ah! You must know your service, you see. You must *know* what each train does and the stations and the sequence they run in. That's why box to box messages are so important – to let people know if there's any "out of course" running. Not just for slips, either. All expresses are "four bells" to us, as you know, and at a place like Didcot the sequence might be the Taunton first and then the Swansea. Say the Taunton is booked to go up the relief line at Foxhall and stop at Didcot while the Swansea goes straight up the main. Then the sequence is reversed down at Wootton Bassett and the signalman there lets the Swansea off the South Wales road in front of the Taunton. The Taunton may be late – well, if he don't tell anyone then Foxhall gets a four bells about the time he's expecting the Taunton, sets the road for the Up relief and the Swansea comes to a grinding halt and has to wait while the signalman swears and finally finds out it's not his Taunton but the Swansea! Whenever you get a boxer message, make sure you pass it on.'

'All right, I will, but what about the slip coaches, how would you go on in a case like that?'

'Like I say, you'd just have to *know*. At the moment there are no slip coaches on the Down line for Didcot or Swindon, and on the Up the only trains with slips are the seven o'clock Weston and 4.55 Fishguard with a coach for Didcot in the mornings and the 1.50 Bristol and 4.40 Weston with coaches for Reading in the afternoon, so it's straightforward – when you are dealing with those trains you expect to see the red/white side-by-side lamp.'

'I used to stand on the platform at Reading and watch the coach separate from the train. I think I'll go and watch it at Didcot.'

'Huh! You won't see much. They slip them at anything up to eighty miles an hour. It's a straight run into the platform, not like on the Up line at Reading, so the guard slips a mile before the station to give himself braking distance. The main train has gone through before the slip arrives.'

'Um, it seems a bit odd, to me, letting a coach go whizzing about all on its own especially over all those junctions near Didcot,' I said hesitantly, rather expecting to be told off for criticising a Great Western speciality.

'It is odd,' agreed Wally warmly, 'and it breaks the basic safety rule – one train at a time on one section of line – when the coach is slipped it makes a second train within one section. It's very good for the passengers because they get an express service to a big junction with connecting service laid on and the railway doesn't have to stop the express, but it is risky, even the rule book recognises that – hold on,' he rummaged in his desk, brought out a thick, blue-covered book and thumbed through it. 'Ah! Here it is, listen. "Where there is a public level-crossing between the place where the slip is made and the station, the crossing must not be fouled until the slip has passed." It makes me smile when I read that but it could be a disaster – the crossing keeper opening the gates after the train has gone by, forgetting about the slip trailing somewhere behind, till Wham! – it goes piling into something on the crossing. You've got to be on your toes when them things are about. By the way, the Down stopper's just off Steventon. Are you going to go home on it?'

'Yes, I think I'd better, so's to be home for dinner.'

'Well, just get the road from Challow for it and pull off down the relief.'

I rang the bell code and then walked towards 58 signal lever. Wally laughed. 'Don't forget we're arse about face here, compared to Challow.' Feeling foolish for forgetting, I went to the opposite end of the frame and pulled point and bolt, 17 and 18 and signals 7, 8, 9, 10. These would have been the Up relief signals at Challow. It did feel odd.

I thanked Wally very much for his long talk and went out, over the tracks, onto the Down platform to buy a ticket. The stern porter was standing in the doorway of the ticket office. I did not see him until I was walking along the platform but realised then that he had seen me walk across the tracks. He might have been a policeman, standing in his clean, blue uniform and he looked at me very steadily, as a policeman would. Large butterflies fluttered in my stomach.

'Trespassing, young man?' he asked quietly.

'I've been to see Wally, Mr Strong,' hoping to show how well in I was, 'and now I've come to buy a ticket to Challow.'

'And making enquiries about me,' he said shrewdly. 'I could have told you who I was if you'd asked. I hope you didn't talk about me for the whole two hours you were up there?' His upper lip was rather long and he seemed to hold it in such a way – as if he was preventing it from curling into a smile. I regained some confidence.

'Wally was telling me about slip coaches and things that go wrong,' I said, hoping to draw him out on the subject of his work at Circourt.

'I see,' he replied, very solemnly, 'and did he tell you' – I thought he was about to tell me his story; I looked at him expectantly and it showed in my face – 'did he tell you', he said again, 'that there was a slip coach here every day but Sunday off a Paddington express from 1874 to 1914 and that the shunting horse and sometimes the tram engine took it back into the siding?'

'No, he didn't. But he did say that all the station staff and the landlord of the Rifle Volunteer were given free travel on the tram.'

'Yes, they were, the old Company were a fair crowd – mind yourself now, here comes the stopper, I must get on but when I see you again I'll expect you to tell me what train carried twenty tail lamps. I'll give you a clue, I saw it every day when I was a strapper.'

He walked away to a four-wheel barrow with a box on it as the train rumbled towards us and called over his shoulder, 'There's no one in the booking office, you'd best jump on the train.'

Back at Challow, Sam said, 'Hi-up then, Ady. Had a good morning?' He did not seem to be worried about my lack of a ticket. 'Yes thanks, Sam. Thanks for getting me on the engine.'

'Nothing to do with me. That was between you and your driver mate. See you again soon.'

'Righto. Tomorrow, I expect.'

Chapter Four

Taking Serge

For nearly three years I went back, riding on the engines and working in the signal box, and because the railwaymen had made their work the focus of their lives, I was not considered eccentric by them but, rather, accepted as an honorary member of the station staff. I left school in December 1955, a month before my fifteenth birthday and after Christmas started looking for a job. The natural course would have been to join the railway but my grandmother sent a pamphlet extolling the benefits of a boys' infantry training unit at Plymouth. My father flatly refused to allow me to join and a fierce battle developed.

I was determined to do as I pleased; I felt sure that the Army must be something pleasant if my father did not want me to join and, if that was not inducement enough, I looked forward to frequent 200-mile-long journeys behind or even upon 'King' class engines and to hearing them working flat out as they climbed over the slopes of Dartmoor. All that and a bright new shilling too.

Mr Halford and Sam were at the station when I arrived with my mother and father to catch the Up stopper for the first part of the Plymouth journey. The train arrived behind 1005 *County of Devon* and we talked at length about the possibilities of the omen. The guard's whistle blew and my father squeezed my hand hard as we parted. 'Good luck, lad,' he said quietly looking straight into my eyes. The short train drew quickly away and I waved back at the little group on the platform, Mum and Dad waving, Sam and Fred Halford standing behind and waving too. I turned to look at the engine, got smuts promptly into both eyes and brought my head inside the compartment, tears pouring down my face. The other people in the compartment stared furtively; I felt terrible but there was no escape in a non-corridor train.

After two years at the Junior Leaders' regiment I became an instructor and realised that, whilst I was technically expert, I was utterly incapable of leading. I took some of the last National Service conscripts through their basic training – the youngest was five years older than me – and muddled along to my own and everyone else's embarrassment for two years. Then, sitting in the barrack room one evening with my latest squad, 'fraternising with the men', I heard someone talking about steam engines. He was a fireman from somewhere in Norfolk and his description of footplate life, told with sincere affection, made me realise my true vocation. I had kept up my connection with Challow station when I was on leave and now, on a weekend off, I went to see Fred Halford. He was as friendly as ever.

'Do you think I could get a job on the railway?' I asked him.

'Bless me, yes!' he replied.

'We could give you a job here straight away but surely you've got to give the Queen a few more years yet?'

'Well yes, officially. But I'm going to see if I can get out sooner.' His face clouded over. 'Look here now, young Adrian, don't go doing anything silly. The Army don't take things like that lightly; you'd get into a miserable fix, you'd upset your parents and don't forget that the railway'll want a good reference before they'd take you on.'

'It's all right, Mr Halford, I've seen some of the glasshouses, you won't find me in one. I'll get an honourable discharge if you're sure I can get a job on the railway.'

'Yes, you can come here. David Castle's just gone up to Wantage as a van driver. I don't suppose anyone else will be after his job here.'

Mr Halford was so keen to help that I did not like to tell him I had no intention of coming to Challow but rather to work on locomotives. The problem now was how to get out of the Army. I spoke to the medical officer about it and he suggested that I developed asthma. During my time as an amateur stable lad in Childrey I had developed an allergic asthma induced by close contact with horses, and as there was a cavalry barracks down the road from our depot, it was easy to bring on crippling attacks of the wheezes; in due course I received my discharge as medically unfit. As I drove away from the barracks, a glorious feeling of freedom surged through me, something, I thought, that no true regular soldier would ever feel.

I underwent an examination by the railway doctor at Park House, Swindon, where a million Great Western men had received similar examinations for a hundred years. After a thorough check the doctor said, 'Well, you appear to be fit, yet your Army discharge was for asthma. What do you want to do on the railway?'

'I'd like to work on the engines.'

'Oh! I can't let you do that. The fumes in the shed and in the Severn tunnel would be very bad for you.' My heart sank under the disappointment. For a few moments the shock made me forget that there were other sorts of railway work and I felt well and truly hoist with mine own petard. Then I remembered Mr Halford's kind offer of a job and Challow box.

'Can I go into a signal box?'

'Certainly, with your asthma that would be the best place,' adding with a smile, 'and I expect you will get a few footplate rides once you get to know the drivers.'

So I went as a Lad Porter to Challow station in September 1960, aged nineteen, till I was old enough to go as a signalman. But even if I had been twenty-one (the

Challow station looking west from the footbridge. Lad Porter Adrian on the left with a parcel for the Down stopping train, Fred Strong on the right. The very plain, red-brick station office dates from 1933 when the Brunel wooden station was demolished during the quadrupling of the line. The steel-framed, breeze-block signal the same. But the 1840, Brunel goods shed survived. When Challow opened – as Faringdon Road – in 1840, it was intended that it should serve Faringdon and Wantage. (H. O. Vaughan, October 1960)

Challow station offices on the Up platform early in 1961. Apart from a garden against the office wall, it appears unchanged since it was rebuilt in 1934.

Westwards of the station office there was a GWR 'Pagoda' corrugated-iron shed where we stored the 40-gallon drums of paraffin for the exterior lighting for the station and the signal lamps. Next to that is the workshop of the Signal & Telegraph Lineman for Challow, Wantage Road and Steventon, John Moody. Across the way is Langford's and Toomer's coal merchants' offices. I never saw Langford's office open but the Toomer office, a brick building, had a weighbridge and a man in charge, John Shepherd. Beyond and behind the Toomer office is the 1910-built house for the station master. A box van stands in the horse and cattle loading bay. (H. O. Vaughan/Author's Collection)

The Didcot–Uffington 'Fly' on 6 January 1957 was hauled by 5639. The loco spotter contingent from Childrey were down at the station to meet it on the way back to Didcot and boarded the engine. Peter Ellis is the one who can be seen in the cab. Others are further inside the cab. It was on the 'Fly' that a Didcot driver coached me, aged twelve, in shunting engine driving. After years of riding on the footplate and watching the working, I quickly picked up the practicalities and became quite expert at batting trucks along the siding with just the right amount of speed and bringing the engine up just so against wagons so that the buffers 'kissed'. (Author)

A busy moment at Challow. The 'Up Fly' has drawn up into the Up platform, shunting, a goods train is passing on the Up main, and on the Down main a 'Castle' is tearing through with the 10.55 a.m. Paddington–Pembroke Dock, the 'Pembroke Coast Express'. I was five days off my sixteenth birthday when I took these on 5 January 1957 and I had only a plastic-bodied, probably with a plastic lens, 'Brownie Cresta' camera. (Author)

The 'Fly Goods' shunting in the yard at Challow. I was coached in driving on engines like this and 5639. (Courtesy Olly Loder)

preferred minimum age), I do not think that the District Inspector would have let me – or anyone – go into a box 'straight off the street' as the saying was. Some sort of probationary period was then considered essential.

I had been told to report to the station at ten o'clock on a Friday morning and drove down the lane full of excitement to be going to work at the place where I had completed a long, childhood association with kind people and fine machines. I mentally compared the friendly familiarity of 'Challer' with the first, bleak night at Plymouth when I was shown into a Victorian barrack room filled with thirty beds and twenty-nine staring strangers – and wondered if Sam Loder would be on duty at the station.

Parking in the yard I entered the station by the parcels office. Mr Halford came out from his inner sanctum and shook my hand. 'I suppose I could say "Welcome back",' he said, with a smile. 'Sam! Come in here a minute – our trained assassin has arrived to protect us.' The door from the platform opened and in came Sam with an ear-to-ear grin, his hand outstretched. 'Hi-up, kid. How's-yer-bum?' He finished very quickly and I was not sure if I had heard him correctly.

'What was that, Sam?'

'Nice bit o' sun.'

'Oh – er – yes,' said I, uncertainly. Mr Halford was keen to get me into uniform. 'Fetch him the spare hat, Sam.' Sam rummaged in a cupboard and came out with a derelict, peaked cap which he jammed on my head. 'Now the passengers will know you're in charge,' he said. 'Right then,' continued Mr Halford, 'we'd better get him measured for his uniform. Let's go into my office where there's more light.'

Straight ahead of me as I came through the door, against the furthest wall, was a row of cupboards extending the width of the room under a single bench top. In the centre was a small, glass window with an oval hole for passing tickets; to the right was a cast-iron date-stamping machine, a tall, wide, pigeonholed rack full of pasteboard tickets; and, leaning back against the cupboards facing me, his elbows resting on the bench top, was Basil, grinning like a Cheshire cat. 'Hello, Adrian. Decided to combine work with pleasure, eh?'

'Of course, you know Basil, don't you,' Mr Halford said to me, 'he's our booking clerk.' Sam turned Quartermaster and spread some forms on the station master's leather-topped desk while Mr Halford picked up an eighteen-inch boxwood ruler marked GWR ready to take my measurements according to Sam's instructions. 'Half arm' and 'half back' was fairly simple, he had some difficulty with 'shoulder to wrist, arm bent' but succeeded in the end by using his finger to keep the place while he moved the ruler. 'Inside leg' was uncomfortable and accompanied by a hoary joke.

'Overcoat or mac?' asked Sam.

'Have the waterproof,' said Mr Halford with a solicitous look.

'No, take the overcoat,' said Sam, 'it's warmer. Those macs are stiff and cold and the collar sticks into your neck when you turn it up in a wind.' I ordered an overcoat. Sam looked down the list of measurements, smiled to himself, glanced up at me and said, 'Well, I suppose they'll be all right. I'll get them on the next Down stopper for Swindon.'

He put the forms in an envelope, took it to the parcels office letter rack, opened the door and went out. I heard him say 'Hi-up, Harry' and saw him pass the windows, apparently going home.

'Isn't Sam on duty then?' I asked.

'Ah – no. He just happened to be around when you arrived,' said Mr Halford. 'Harry, come in here and meet your learner.' Harry came in looking exactly the same as he looked four years before. 'Do you know Adrian?'

'Yes, Mr Halford. We have met.' He said, looking across at me and nodding in a friendly way. 'He's come to work here then, has he?'

'Yes, he'll be with you until you've shown him the ropes and he can manage on his own.'

'That'll be all right. I must get on now, there's some stuff for the Up stopper to see to.'

There was a knock on the oak slide in front of the ticket window and Basil lifted it, bending slightly. On the other side a face appeared as if its owner was lying on his side as he looked through the glass. A passenger was bowing from the waist – a supplicatory posture that the Great Western would have considered no more than correct – asking for a ticket. 'Cheap day to Reading, please.' Basil took his money, flicked a ticket from the rack, got change and slid the money and pasteboard through the little, oval hole with a cheerful, 'Thanks very much.' The passenger grunted something, taken aback perhaps by Basil's manner, and moved away. 'Cheerful cove,' said Basil. 'Haven't seen him before. I wonder what he's on.'

A telephone on the wall rang the stopping train code – 3-1. 'That's the Up stopper just leaving Uffington; the signalman rings the telephone to warn us. Come on, we'll go out to the platform.'

The train arrived behind a shiny 'County' class engine, just out of the factory. Harry put some boxes in with the guard, took a parcel off, made sure the passengers' door was shut and waved to the guard. The guard gave 'Right Away' and within a minute of its arrival the train was on its way again. Harry went immediately to his office, Basil slipped off to the signal box for his coffee and Mr Halford led me along the platform. 'You know your way around the station. I'll take you out to the power points and show you what to do if they go wrong.'

We strolled along the platform on a warm, comfortable September day while he told me about the station. 'In spite of those four tracks up there making the place look like the outer suburbs of London, Challow is a country station and depends on the villages for its support. There's no big centre of population to help us. The atmosphere is like on a branch line; we have a stopping service connecting with the junction at Didcot and Swindon and one express to London in the morning and another back at night. Those express trains going through the middle roads are really nothing to do with us and you soon learn to take no notice of them.' I did not believe I would ever come to ignore them but said nothing. 'We have a good following of regular passengers – we know them all by sight, some by name and *they* know us. Some of them come to Challow in preference to a station closer to their home because they appreciate the service we give them. The passengers are our bread and butter and the first rule in the book, as far as I am concerned, says to be "prompt, civil and obliging". I hope you will remember that and not let the station down.'

Although he said all this with the utmost seriousness, he seemed glad to change the subject. 'The lines through here were quadrupled during 1932 and '33; before that, it was ordinary double track – the present Up relief and Up main lines used to be the Up and Down mains – there was an old Up goods loop but that came out in 1933. You can see the space it occupied on the left of the Up relief all covered in bushes. Albert Stanley has his chicken run on it. Have you met Albert yet?' I said I had not. 'You must have seen him. He lives in the station terrace and goes out every evening to feed his chickens – he's a well-built man with quite a ruddy face and close-cropped grey hair.'

'I know who you mean. He always walks with a collie at his heels.'

'That's the man. Come down the platform ramp. There's the 63 ¾ mile post from Paddington – Albert and Harry are the best men I've ever worked with; they're both old hands. Harry started at Woodborough in 1916 and Albert started at Dauntsey about 1920, I think.

'Now, here are the power points and there is one of the motors you turn with the hurdy-gurdy; the other motor is at the other end of the turn-out. If the signalman can't get the points over on the motor, he'll call you. Go to the box for the hand crank. It's like a wheel nut spanner for a motor car and it's padlocked into a contact box on the instrument shelf of the signal box. Once you take the hand crank out, you lock all point and signal levers relevant to the set of points you're working on, so get it back to the signal box and into the contact box as soon as you can when you've finished with it. Don't forget to take a red and green flag and a point clip, padlock and key as well. When you get to the points, have a look between the movable blade of the points and the rail at both ends to see if there is anything preventing the blades from closing, a stone or bit of grit, but if you can't see anything, you'll have to wind the points over by hand till the lineman can come to put them right.

'Take the cover off here. There, you see that squared end? You put the crank mouth over it and turn till the points are reversed. Don't forget to wind both ends of the turn-out, facing and trailing. Then you must put a clamp on the blade at the facing end and screw it up tight against the rail and padlock the handle so that the vibration of the train cannot unscrew it. Do you know what I mean by "facing" end?'

'The end where the train first meets the points.'

'Right. That's the dangerous end. If the blades are not closed up tight against the rail the train will come off the road. If the trailing end is wrong, the train will smash the rodding and the motor but at least it won't derail.'

Railway work immediately took on a more serious aspect for me – I felt nervous at the very thought of moving points by hand and at all this talk of derailments and resolved to be very wary. I could imagine myself being so careful in making the facing end safe that I would forget about moving the trailing end and thus be responsible for smashing up hundreds of pounds' worth of equipment.

'When you've got the points turned and clamped,' Mr Halford continued, 'go over to that telephone by the Down relief inner home and tell the signalman and then work under his instructions. When he wants you to let a train pass over the points, you will stand at the facing end and hold out your green flag.'

We stepped back onto the path just as a man I took to be Albert Stanley emerged from the bushes, a bucket over his arm, a dog at his heels.

'Good morning, Mr Halford, nice day,' he said in a gentle Wiltshire voice.

'Hello, Albert. Have you met Adrian?'

'No, I can't say I have. Is he starting on the railway?'

'Yes, he'll be on with Harry first thing Monday at seven o'clock.'

'Well, I hope you enjoy the job. It's a quiet little number and you couldn't have a better teacher than Harry.'

I liked Albert immediately. Somehow his voice sounded cheerful and optimistic and he looked like the classic countryman, straightforward and honest with blue eyes and broad shoulders, standing solidly on the path in his wellingtons, his dog to heel, tongue lolling, smiling at the world.

An Up express came into earshot and then into sight. It was 'Castle'-hauled and travelling unusually fast, the thrilling, thudding, rapid tiff-tiff-tiff-tiff of a locomotive 'notched up and flying', growing louder by the second till it was suddenly drowned by a crescendo of rail noise as the wheels thundered past our little group, shaking the very ground we stood on. I had watched trains for years and loved them – now that I was going to have some very small part to play in controlling them, I was a little bit afraid.

'My goodness, they were going well,' Albert said appreciatively, staring after the train.

'A good eighty, I should think,' said Mr Halford. 'Shall we go back to the station?' We moved towards the platform. 'When I was a young porter I had a very fast ride down Honeybourne bank – over four miles downhill at one in a hundred – I reckon we touched a hundred at the bottom. I was on early turn at Blockley sometime in 1932 and travelled home to Evesham each day by train with my bike in the van. Well, on this occasion the train ran into Blockley; I knew the driver by sight and he waved me up to the engine. "Do you want to ride with us, Fred?" he says. Of course I was all for it, put my bike in the van and then hopped up on the engine. "How fast shall we go down the bank?" this driver says and like a fool I said, "I bet you can't manage a hundred." "I wouldn't want to take advantage of your youth," he says and turns to his fireman. "Hey mate, Fred here doesn't reckon we can do a hundred down Honeybourne." Well, the fireman just laughed, the guard gave "Right" and off we went.

'They had a "Saint" and they opened her up so hard that I fell back against the tender – she had only six coaches – and I then I realised they weren't joking. They were building up as high a speed as possible before the start of the downhill run.

I looked at my watch as we passed Chipping Campden – it said 2.38. We were going great guns there; it's uphill but you wouldn't have thought so and I began to worry about the long bank ahead – it wasn't even a straight run downhill but curved this way and that.

'We tipped over the summit, I'm not exaggerating, I felt the engine go, the trees at the lineside just became a blur and I travelled down wedged tight in the front corner of the cab, looking along the boiler and watching it heeling to the canted curves like a ship on a stormy sea. At the foot of the bank was Honeybourne station with facing junction, crossovers and all sorts of point work. I just about bit my tongue as we hit them, the engine seemed to jump into the air and come crashing down, the noise was deafening and we were swaying still from that enormous crash as we came up to the station or rather the station came out to meet us. I thought we'd hit the platforms but we'd steadied by that time and we went straight in, whistle wide open. The footbridge just didn't look high enough – I ducked instinctively as we went under it. There was one more crash as we passed over some more junctions at the far end of the station and we were clear.

'My goodness, they frightened me! And even then the cranky old devil didn't slow up. I barely saw Littleton & Badsey and I'd just begun to think he'd gone out of his mind as Aldington Sidings distant signal came tearing up to us along the track when he slammed the brakes on and almost before I knew it we were grinding to a halt in Evesham station.

'When I got down off the engine, my knees were like jelly and I couldn't walk straight. My ears were ringing too but I heard him laughing, saying, "Hey, young Fred, what's the time?" I'd forgotten that and looked at my watch – 2.46 – and told him. "How fast is that then?" says he, with a stupid great grin. I told him I'd work it out and tell him next day and went off to get my bike from the van. I never bothered to go home on the engine again. Well, not on that bit of line. We'd taken just less than eight minutes from passing Campden to stopping in Evesham, which was an average speed of just over eighty so we may have touched a hundred at Honeybourne.'

'The mad devils,' growled Albert, ''t'isn't railway work, is it? I s'pose they were Cockneys.'

'No, I think they were Oxford men.' We had arrived back at the station and Mr Halford turned to go to his office.

'Right then, Adrian. Be here on Monday at first light, or even before, seven o'clock on, with Harry Strong.'

Chapter Five

Cheltenham Ceremony

Next morning I got out of bed at six o'clock with an alarm clock clattering reveille. When I got downstairs and went to the kitchen to make some tea, intending to sit quiet for a while until I felt alive, I found my mother making my breakfast – a hearty one would describe it well. I could not face it but drank some tea and managed to slip away when she was not looking, and was on the road at 6.40 in my 1935 Morris Eight saloon.

Twenty-five-year-old cars may sound like trouble to car drivers now but in 1960 there were a great many stalwart pre-war cars on the roads. My Morris was a simple, reliable car. She had no heater, no suspension (only leaf springs), her headlamps were about as much use as candles but I loved her. She had a solid, rust-free body on a proper chassis that still carried Lord Nuffield's black enamel paint. Her hydraulic brakes were first class and she had a cruising speed of 35/40 mph on a smooth road, the power coming from a side-valve engine, which ran like the proverbial sewing machine.

Dawn was splitting the night sky when I got to the station at 6.50. It was strange to see the place dark and deserted but I had hardly a minute to contemplate this novelty before I heard the sound of a Bantam two-stroke popping sedately up the hill from Stanford-in-the-Vale. Shortly afterwards Harry appeared, riding very upright and going very slowly so as not to get mud or dust on his shiny, black boots.

He dismounted, pulled the machine onto its stand without a word to me and as I hovered nervously behind him he fitted a key into the parcels office doors, turned it and entered, switching the lights on with his right hand as he did so. I followed him in.

'Good morning, Harry.'

'Good morning, young man,' he murmured, handing me his bunch of keys. 'This one's for the station master's door and this is for the door to the platform and these two are for the doors at each end of the booking hall. Just go round and open up if you please.'

I managed the first two but let the other keys slip. Harry was slowly unbuttoning his railway-issue macintosh and looked preoccupied. I did not dare disturb his thoughts so went out onto the dark platform and fumbled in the lock of the booking hall door with every key on the bunch before I found the right one. The other door, by luck, I opened quickly and went back to the office.

Harry was now sitting on a big wooden drum marked 'Artificial Insemination Officer. Faringdon. Solidified Carbon Dioxide'. He had removed one brown legging and was in the process of removing the other. It was a complicated procedure because it was suspended by a strap fixed to the buttons to which his braces were attached. The unbuttoning and rebuttoning was being carried out by feel alone as he sat gazing thoughtfully through the office window. Once released, the legging was drawn off carefully, folded and the pair put on a shelf. Each clip was gently removed, the folded cloth smoothed, he stood up and stamped each polished ankle-length boot to make sure the creases were falling straight.

While this was going on I stood helplessly and looked around. On the platform side of the room was a tabletop running from the door to the wall that divided the office from the station master's room. A high stool was provided to enable the porter to sit at the table and a large window illuminated his work. Against the dividing wall was a rack containing ledgers, waybill forms, glue pots, labels and all the paraphernalia of an office. A stove stood in the centre of this transverse wall and on its chimney breast was a mass of dusty paper, old notices and posters. There was a 'Pooley' weighing scale and a big rack for parcels. I had not thought of railway work in the context of an office and stared at the incomprehensible jumble, looked out at the grey tracks and gloomy platform and wondered where the romance was.

Harry had a lot of what the Army called 'personal pride'. He was of medium height, slim, with well-groomed silver hair like many a railwayman, but where other men were tidy in their uniforms, Harry was sheer elegance – and elegance in railway-issue blue serge was very nearly impossible. It was obvious that his wife took as much pride in his appearance as he did himself for his jacket and trousers showed signs of frequent brushings with a stiff brush and frequent ironings with a hot iron. His shirt and collar were crisp and white, worn with a dark blue tie and now he was going to book on duty and bring this pride to the service of the railway.

He signed on duty for 7 a.m. at 6.55, I signed beneath his name and then he spoke. 'Right. Now we must change the date stamp.' I followed him and watched while he took the ancient machine apart. A pin appeared in his hand at a thought, he used it to pick out a piece of leaden type, the pin vanished into his lapel, he selected the new figure from a box of type, put the machine together, folded a piece of paper and tried the stamp – all a series of well-tried actions, moving like clockwork. 12 SEP 60. 'Good. Follow me.'

I blundered out behind him, wondering how I should read typeface when it was upside down and back to front; indeed, I felt as if I was a piece of type. The Army had a phrase for it, referring to something or other being 'spare at a wedding'. We went into the waiting room where a fire was already laid in the grate. 'The late turn man does this for you,' he said as he produced a box of matches and set the paper alight. 'Follow me.' We went out onto the platform.

'We don't really need the Tilleys; it's getting light but in a week or so we'll have to put them out so I'll just show you how they work.' He selected yet another key from his bunch, released a padlock on the door of a corrugated-iron hut with a curved roof and stepped inside. It was dark there but I could see some big, paraffin-burning lamps hanging in rows, seven on each side of the hut. Almost at once the clammy chill of the place made itself felt and I listened, covered in goosepimples, as Harry explained:

'You put meths into this dish holding the wick around the vaporising tube and light it.' He took a can of meths. 'On the darkest mornings we put only three lamps out, just around the station office, but at night there's trains on the downside too and you must put all the lamps out right round the station; there's one here for each post. Now I'll pressurise the fuel tank.' His fingers landed directly on a bicycle pump, which was invisible in the gloom, and connected it to a valve. 'You pump until this little indicator comes up a bit; it doesn't need much – there that'll do. Now, don't turn the fuel tap on too soon; give the meths time to heat the vaporising tube – just before the methylated goes out is the best time. If you try it too soon you'll get raw paraffin all over the place, smoke and fumes and you'll blacken the glass globe.'

We stood and waited while the methylated spirit burned down. I looked out of the hut at the grey, misty morning, when the sun came up it might even be pretty, shining through the mist till it was dispersed but at that moment it was miserably foggy with a touch of frost. I felt a yawn coming on, tried to hide it from Harry and wished I could get out of that dismal hut. The meths was still burning strongly.

'I was here when they tested these lamps in 1923,' Harry volunteered, 'acceptance trials I suppose you'd call them. The Company reckoned they saved £3 in a year here in paraffin so they made a bulk order with Tilleys. Look, they're called "Challow" lamps.'

'Did they worry about £3 a year?' I asked, the cold freezing manners.

'Don't forget there were thousands of stations and tens of thousands of lamps. These Tilleys give a far brighter light than the old wick lamps so they used less paraffin and fewer lamps. The old Company had to keep its shareholders happy. They had to make a profit and there was no one to bail them out if they didn't so they were careful with their housekeeping. We've still got the sieve the Company issued us to take bits of unburnt coal from the ashes before we throw them away –'

'Phew, that's a bit miserly, isn't it?'

'Oh no 'tisn't either. I can see you're not a householder. Years ago everyone sieved their ashes. You could waste a couple of pounds of coal else. You may as well throw money away. And the Company expected us to look after their property as if it was our own.'

The methylated spirit had burned low now, Harry turned the handle and the gas popped into life, hissing in the mantle, incandescent yellow. It reminded me of the gas light in my grandmother's living room but less bright. 'Now it's going, and not before, you can pump the tank up really hard', said Harry, working vigorously, 'till the indicator is sticking up well above its casing.' The light changed to a brilliant white. He took it outside and winched it onto a tall mast by the platform gate. 'We won't do any more now because it's getting light. But remember – put your lamps out at the proper time and the proper number or else. If someone falls and hurts themselves on an unlit station, the Company is responsible.'

As Harry was winding the lamp up, the first passenger came into the yard, appearing out of the mist, black and featureless at first, riding a bicycle. 'That's old Joe, Joe Tilling, coming for the stopper to Steventon. He's early turn crossing keeper at Causeway,' said Harry. There was something strange about him that I could not fathom for a moment and then I realised he was cycling with one leg only, the other hanging unnaturally stiff and useless, an artificial leg. The bike had what was called a 'fixed wheel'.

'How far has he come?' I asked Harry.

'Up from Stanford, about three miles. Poor old Joe, he lost his leg in an accident at work years ago and they gave him the crossing job at Causeway.'

Joe heaved himself off his bicycle and wheeled it slowly through the gateway. He was a tall, gaunt man with a hooked nose on a long, pain-stretched face which looked worse for the mouth being slightly open. He was having difficulty in breathing and could only gasp, as he passed, 'Mornin', Harry – fog's bad.' He went a few paces along the platform and stopped, leaning over the saddle of his machine to get his breath back.

'He looks ill,' I said.

'Old Joe doesn't give up easily,' replied Harry almost proudly as he walked back to the parcels office. 'Doesn't matter what shift he's on he'll be there. They work their shifts to suit him where they can and he gets there even if he cycles the whole way. To make sure of it in weather like this he just starts earlier.'

'Who else will there be for the stopper?'

'Only Jimmy Titchener, the district lampman – Basil's father – and a couple of building labourers for Reading and they've got season tickets.'

A cheerful, wind-blown face, brown and lined, looked round the door just then, grinned and brought the rest of the body into the office. 'Hi-up, 'Arry. Raw cold this morning and you 'aven't lit the fire. I'll have to go in the waiting room with the nobs.'

'Who's in there then, Jimmy?'

'Oh, only a couple of blokes. You've got a mate then; blind leading the blind is it?'

'Not quite,' said Harry, just a tiny bit stiffly. 'This is our learner.'

'Oh-ah. Our Basil has mentioned you, nice to meet you, you're going to be a signalman, I hear.' I felt embarrassed at that – it sounded as if I was going about boasting about an imminent promotion. Just at that moment in my career it seemed the height of presumption to even think about being a signalman.

'Er, I think I'll have to get the hang of this job first,' I mumbled.

Just then Bill in the signal box rang the 3-1 code on the station telephone circuit and we moved outside to wait for the train. Jimmy Titchener was small of stature, dressed in the same uniform as Harry but the cloth was coarse, stained and weatherbeaten. Beneath his waistcoat he wore a scuffed flannel shirt, open at the neck in all weathers, and sticking out from under his shapeless, baggy trouser legs were a pair of hob-nailed boots, their toes turned up from a great deal of walking. He had at his feet a two-gallon can of paraffin with a long, thin, curving spout and six signal lamps on a wooden carrying bar.

I had seen him at work and seen his slight figure, far away along the track, trudging home at the end of a day's work and I knew that he was no small man but a tough and determined one. His district began at Steventon and extended to Marston Crossing West's Up distant signal nineteen miles to the west and as his signal lamps held seven days' supply of fuel he had to cover the area in a strict seven-day rota. If he did not there would be a lot of signals without lights and many delays to trains as a result so that no matter what the weather he had to keep up with his timetable. In summer sun or winter rain, on the appointed day, the signalman would expect to see Jimmy trudging over the ballast with his can in one hand and his bar of fresh lamps in the other.

As a schoolboy I had watched him go from signal post to ground disc, scrambling up twenty- or thirty-foot-high ladders, often in winds that swayed their posts alarmingly, carrying new lamps for old. Once on the lamp platform he replaced the time-expired lamp and lit the fresh one. Expertise was required to do this in a light breeze – it seemed impossible in a gale but he held the matchstick as far from the head as possible, the matchbox dose over the hole in the top of the lamp case. Then he struck downwards, straight and accurate onto the wick while the phosphorus was still flaring. He adjusted the lamp wick to the size of his smallest finger nail and the lamp was set fair for another seven days. Occasionally, a particularly violent storm might blow a lamp out but nothing that was in Jimmy's power to do was left undone in ensuring that trains on the Didcot–Swindon line ran under bright, clear signals.

The train ran into the station with only two coaches, the engine stopping by the parcels office door, infinitely more desirable than the stuff of a porter's life but I felt bound by Harry and resisted the temptation to go up and look at it. The two railwaymen got in with the guard, he and Harry helping Joe up. I was motioned to see to the labourers; I closed their door behind them and raised my arm in the approved manner, the guard blew his whistle and away went the train. Having raised my arm, having actually done something, I felt a little more cheerful.

The Up stopper withdrew to reveal the Down parcels train waiting at the far platform.

'That's the 5.5 Padd,' said Harry, tossing a bundle of notices onto the office table. We went over the footbridge and found the train guard waiting in front of an open van door. 'Bring that four-wheel barrow,' commanded Harry.

'Got a helper, mate? I reckon you'll need one for this lot.' We had piled two barrows with parcels and boxes before the train left.

'Now then,' said Harry, 'these must go in the lock-up in the down-side waiting room until the lorry comes to collect them – except for any marked for collection here, they must come over to our office. You'll have to enter details of consignor, consignee and ledger label number on a delivery sheet and then again in the parcels inwards book. I'll go and get the sheets and I'll give you a hand.' My heart sank as I looked at the monotonous piles in the damp, grey light ...

While we were drudging away, turning over the boxes to find the side with the information, the Fly arrived and Harry went off to see the guard. A goods train went clattering down the main line, past the local goods before he returned. 'I've told the guard that there is nothing to pick up so he may as well put the coal off when he comes back from Uffington, that'll save crossing over now. That was the Hinksey just gone down the main, so the Fly'll go now. You'll have to ask the guard to help himself in the yard at this time of day – if there is anything for downhill, tell him where it is and let him fetch it without your assistance. I must go now to be in the booking office in case anyone comes for the 8.5 – you have to keep everything in mind – don't get bogged down in this job and forget about a train that's due and let someone go without a ticket.' The Fly started up with a savage tug of coupling links as he walked away. I had not even seen who the driver was. I finished at eight o'clock and went to the office with the sheets; there were about fifty entries.

'Enter them up now,' said Harry. 'Here's some tea. I've sold three tickets for Paddington while you were over there so just remember what I told you. You'll have to drop the parcels job and get back here and if you haven't got it all entered when old Fred turns up with his lorry, he'll have to wait for you.'

The 8.5 Swindon to Paddington 'semi-fast' left just as the parcels lorry arrived on the down-side and I hurried over with Harry to load it. Some girls were arriving too; instead of thinking whether they were pretty or not, I just thought 'Oh! There must be another train!' Harry left after five minutes to 'watch the shop' leaving me with the caustic old lorry driver. I could not imagine me telling him to 'wait while I finish my entries'. Nothing I did was right for him and he soon reduced me to a state of confused immobility. 'Er ... I think I'll go and meet the Down train.' He did not reply, so I slunk away. Waiting in the shelter were three girls, one of about twelve but the others were sixteen or seventeen, one with red hair, the other with auburn. 'Morning.' I was not even sure myself whether this was an announcement or a greeting. They smiled awkwardly and the train arrived to save us all. Harry appeared in time to give 'Right' to the guard, the guard gave 'Right Away' to the driver and the train left in a smother of steam.

'The lorry is on the up-side now. Fred's waiting for you to make up your ledger; you'd better hurry over there,' said Harry, and I went over the footbridge yet again. While I was writing, eating a sandwich at the same time, Mr Halford arrived with some sarcasm about people who have nothing to do all day but sit around eating. He was quickly followed by Basil, who never left his breakfast table in the station terrace until he had seen his boss walk past.

During the Great Western Railway's centenary dinner in 1935 the Prince of Wales had called the Company 'The Royal Road' for its long association with Windsor and the Royal Family, and since that time supervisory staff had worn buttons bearing the Company's initials surmounted by the imperial crown. Mr Halford still wore his 'Royal' buttons twelve years after nationalisation; he knew why they bore the crown and was determined to keep up the Great Western tradition of style and service. Having entered his office he took out his *very smart hat*, put it on and went out to patrol the car park, ready to welcome the *very smart people*, who were about to arrive for the 8.58 'to Town'. I do not think they ever went 'to London' in those days though occasionally they mentioned '*Peddington*'. The ritual of the 'Cheltenham' was about to begin.

Almost in convoy the cars arrived – a Rolls-Royce perhaps, some Rovers, a Morris Thousand station wagon and maybe Major Sneyd's misfiring V8 Pilot – crunching over the gravel, pulling up in a queue to discharge their passengers. Mr Halford took his dictum 'the passengers are our bread and butter' seriously and welcomed each one by name when he knew it, and certainly by a cheerful 'Good morning'. 'Good morning, Sir John', 'Good morning, my lord' popped off here and there among the lesser 'Good morning, ma'am' or 'sir'. They were ushered into the waiting room by Harry; I heard cries of 'Oh! What a lovely fire', though very special guests were entertained in Mr Halford's own office. The people seemed to know each other very well, good nature abounded and conversation thrived. Their train was the 7.5 a.m. Cheltenham to Paddington express, hauled by a Gloucester-based 'Castle'. It arrived at the platform whereupon Mr Halford, Basil and Harry performed a flurry of door opening, ushering and door slamming. I noticed, too, that Harry touched his cap each time he opened the door and seemed to touch the hands of some of the passengers as if he was saying goodbye to them. I was standing in the office doorway and could not see properly but it was an odd gesture.

Having seen everyone into the train Harry then walked the length of the coaches, checking that all doors were secure, till he got to the engine; then, he swung round and raised his right arm to signal that all was in order. Mr Halford then wheeled smartly about and raised *his* right arm to the guard – who was not more than six feet away – to signify that the train was in order. The guard blew his whistle with enthusiasm and waved his green flag with a fine flourish. At that, Mr Halford executed his military about-turn and signalled to Harry, who whirled about and signalled to the fireman – who had already seen the guard's flag – that it was all right to start. 'Right Away!' cried the fireman to his mate, who replied with a toot on the whistle, and in a climax of ritual, the big 'Castle' barked away from the platform, 420 tons in tow, as majestically as you could wish.

Having observed all the correct forms and kept the Company spirit alive for another day, Mr Halford changed his very smart hat for an ordinary hat and went to the signal box for a cup of coffee with Bill Mattingley.

Chapter Six

Harry Remembers

Harry drank his tea with his cap on standing up. Basil slipped away quietly to the booking office taking his tea with him. I wanted to sit down but the only seat was the high stool, too conspicuous, so I compromised by leaning against the table.

'Well, young man, do you think you'll like it here?'

'I suppose I shall when I get the hang of what we're doing.'

'You mustn't be confused yet; you haven't started. Basil has got to show you the booking side of things because you'll be in charge of the station every evening after 4.30. Basil will confuse you if you let him.'

'Thanks very much,' came floating out of the other room. Harry's upper lip quivered as he had a little smile to himself. 'Drink up quick, mind. We want to be down the yard to see what's on before the Fly comes. They're always back from Uffington quick on a Monday and we must see what wants knocking out of the yard.'

There was the noise of a lorry which I took to be going over the road bridge. 'Hi-up! There's a lorry in the yard. We're early today.' He took a final mouthful of tea and went out with me following like Albert Stanley's collie dog. I wanted to know why the train was called the Fly but it seemed a frivolous question to ask Harry so I shelved the matter by thinking 'It's because it dodges about from place to place.' I realised that he was telling me something. 'All these cars pay a fee to park here. One and sixpence a day or half a crown in either of the lock-ups.' There were three garages.

'What's wrong with the third shed?'

'Mr Halford keeps *his* car in it.'

In front of us, at the far side of a wide gravel yard with a derelict, rubber-tyred crane and what appeared to be a grounded wagon body, was a lorry-load of straw bales standing in the archway of the big old goods shed. We passed the crane and skirted the wagon that was, in fact, on rails below yard-level, an appendix from the through siding, and reached the lorry. It was Oakley's of Alvescot.

'Good morning, driver,' said Harry.

'Whatcher mate.' I winced at the irreverence. 'Straw for yer jersey. Where d'ye want it?'

'You can put it in the wagon in Goosey Dock,' replied Harry, emphasising 'you' and pointing to the appendix track.

The man looked as if he was going to protest. Maybe he wanted us to help him load but after a second glance at Harry, whose upper lip was now in the 'determined' position while the rest of him looked like a policeman, he slammed his cab door and took it out on the clutch as he backed up to the wagon. 'Look out for lorry drivers,' said Harry, as we watched the lorry go backwards in a series of leaps and bounds, 'they'll have you doing their work and you'll be neglecting your own.'

A whitewashed brick hut with piles of coal behind it, a weighbridge in front and a board on its roof saying JOHN TOOMER & SONS LTD was close by, and out of it now came a stout, red-faced man, smiling broadly. 'Morning, Harry. Not a bad day now. Is the Fly about? We've got some coal on order.'

'There's two on there for you Frank. It ought to be here any time now.'

'Thanks, I'll go and get the men and the lorry ready. Got a mate, I see?' He turned to me and beamed rosily again.

'Yes, he'll be in charge here soon. Adrian, this is Frank Shepherd, Toomer's agent.'

'Pleased to meet you, Mr Shepherd,' I said, stupidly trying to puzzle out why it said 'Toomer' over his office, embarrassed by Harry's expression of confidence in me.

'Where are you from? I don't think I've seen you before.'

'I've just arrived from the Army. You deliver to my parents, next to the Crown in Childrey.'

'Ah! I know, very nice people.' His cheeks were red as rear lamps. 'I'll see you again then.'

He turned back to his office. Harry and I walked through Brunel's gothic arch into the cavernous goods shed. We climbed up some steps onto an ancient timber platform about fifteen feet wide running the length of the building, perhaps fifty yards, beside a double line of rails, which I thought was an unusual feature in a country goods shed. Harry went into the goods shed office and left me admiring the huge timbers spanning the walls from which great joists rose lesser beams, fanlike, to support the purlins and rafters. Once they had all been painted white, and though the paint was greyed and flaking, they were still white enough to be seen even in the gloom of the roof's ridge, perhaps fifty feet above my head. The proportions were ecclesiastical and I found it difficult to imagine the flood of traffic through the place which must once have existed to warrant such a building.

Harry emerged with a shunting pole in his hand and saw me gazing round.

'It's a fine building. Brunel didn't stint the timber. They must be whole, seasoned oaks up there,' he said, looking up with me.

'Yes, it's a lovely place, but why is it so big? Whatever sort of traffic did they have out here in the Vale?'

'Well, when it was built, Challow was called "Faringdon Road" and was the station for Wantage *and* Faringdon from 1840 to 1845, and until 1864 it was the station for Faringdon – till they built the branch from Uffington.'

'Which is when the name was changed to Challow, I suppose?'

'Yes, so you see there must have been very heavy traffic here because anything that moved in those days went by rail.' We walked down the platform, our footsteps hollow and echoing in the vast old barn.

'There's the old stable – I used to have a lovely horse in there, called her Duchess. That was early days for me, about 1924. She was the shunting horse and could walk between the rails – lots of 'em couldn't – and even reverse with a wagon. She used to stop work when a train went by and watch it with her ears pricked up, wonderful horse, but she was killed by an engine in the end. Well, the vet shot her but it was because an engine hit her.'

'That must have been horrible for you. But tell me, was there so much work here that you needed a horse to be shunting trucks around all the time? Why was it so busy?'

'Bless my soul! Work? Ha! Ha! T'wasn't always like it is now, you know. There was three milk-empty trains and two milk-loaded trains and two Flys, besides the stoppers – and that was just on Sunday,' he rose to a triumphant crescendo as he produced his surprise.

We were strolling along a line of wagons then, covered vans and coal trucks, loaded and empty. 'See that empty siding between this one and the Up relief line? That would have been full of traffic like this right up to the end of the last war. We had a staff of five porters here then, three or four of us through the day and one or two all night. There was Harry Crooks, I remember. He went as lampman to Bath and was killed on the line soon after. Then there was Tom Gillman and Reg Chester ... But look here,' he brought the subject back abruptly to work, 'we must book the wagons in and out, and any that spend more than three days in the siding must pay a fine – demurrage – it always makes a row but we have to do it.'

The Fly arrived at that moment and we waited for the guard to come up. He walked along in an odd way; something was wrong but I couldn't think what.

He was barrel-shaped, scruffy and cheerful looking with two days' stubble on his chin.

''Lo 'Arry, yuh long streak o' misery! We've got *four* o' coal for yuh now, picked up two off the Faringdon to go with what we already 'ad and there's four empty opens for yuh. Can't say we don't look after yuh, eh? Ha! Ha!'

Harry seemed to draw back from this geniality and stood several feet away very upright with his pole at what I could call the 'Carry' in contrast to the guard who appeared to be using his as a crutch. 'Very good,' clipped out Harry. 'I have six empty tubs and two box vans to knock out and I'll have the four opens inside the goods shed. That's all.' The way he delivered the last two words made me wonder if he was dismissing the guard or if he meant that that was the extent of the shunting required.

The engine was a pannier tank; its driver and fireman I did not know, and they drove forward on the guard's handsignal with part of the train, the last wagons of the string being the 'Challows'. Once clear of the hand points, the train set back into the siding and was coupled to the row of wagons by Harry using his pole

Harry Strong. Harry drove the Challow shunting horse *Duchess*. Here he is with his horse in 1924 – about the same as in this picture as when I went to work with him, aged nineteen, in 1960. (Courtesy of the late Harry Strong)

No. 6826 *Nannerth Grange* ex-works on a 'running-in' turn, arriving at Challow with the 10.55 Swindon–Didcot on 1 July 1958. Mr Halford is on the right, Fred Strong, the Steventon crossing keeper, is walking to collect his bike. I can't recall the name of the porter on the left. (H. O. Vaughan/Author's Collection)

dextrously to flick the heavy links over the draw-hook. It looked easy enough, and I looked forward to trying my hand at what seemed to me more like railway work than copying numbers off sticky labels.

The whole 'raft' was then drawn out over the points and the job of sorting the empties from the loadeds began, banging one empty 'onto the van', the next batch of loadeds into the siding whence they came: Harry did the uncoupling and gave stop/go signs to the driver while the guard leant on the hand point lever and tugged it – rather inexpertly I thought and wished I could do it; once he nearly fell over – to change the route as required: 'van-side' or 'siding'. At last the new arrivals were pushed onto the siding and as the pannier tank went back onto its train, Harry was taking wagon numbers.

'That guard was odd,' I ventured.

'Odd? He was tipsy!' snorted Harry. 'Some of these guards go into the Junction at Uffington and have a pint but he'd been on the hard stuff.'

'Does it happen very often?'

'Not like that. Some of the guards on the Fly have a pint out of hours but I've never seen him like that before. When I was a young lad I knew two or three old guards and porters that used to get quite tipsy on duty but everyone always covered for them. It's unusual nowadays.' He changed the subject.

'I have the stour of the yard now, what's here and what's gone away. All the details must be phoned through to Swindon and that's the time you ask for empty wagons. Nelson's haven't been in for a few days with one of their fancy trailers so we must expect them soon. We'll order a flat truck for them and a couple more opens – they'll come up on Wednesday. Always bear your customers in mind and try to have a wagon there when they want it but don't waste a wagon by just hoarding it.'

I felt depressed at this because I didn't even know who our customers were. Harry supplied the answer. 'There's few enough of them. Nelson over at Cross Bargains farm makes a special trailer for hay bales and has to have a flat truck, maybe three a week. W & G's of East Challow make farm equipment in wood, like pig-houses and hay-racks; they usually have opens for loading – oh, and they also bring down thousands of telephone pole crossbars, filthy things, all freshly creosoted. Then there's this seasonal hay and straw and next January and February there'll be sugar beet – we use coal tub empties for that. And that's it. You'll be kept busy by it but it's only just enough work for one man. Now let's show you how to use a shunting pole.'

The pole was an ash stick about 6 feet long, 1 ½ inches thick, shod at one end with a steel ferrule ending in a curly hook like a pig's tail.

'Now,' said Harry, 'first off, I'll show you how to pin down a hand-brake. The pole's not supposed to be used for this but it always has been. You must lever the hand-brake handle down hard with the pole and slip the pin in over the top to hold it. Then, when you want to let the brake off, you ease the handle off the pin with the shunting pole, take out the pin and there you are. Always put the handle up onto its rest, or the brake-block will be juddering on the wheel and driving the guard mad.

'To uncouple, just put the pole over the buffer stock, rest the ferrule against the draw-hook underneath the coupling and lever it off – so. To couple up pick the link up in the ferrule hook and swing the pole upwards and forwards – so twisting the wrists to empty the link out of the hook, over the draw-bar hook. You try it now.'

I picked up a shunting pole for the first time and found it thick and clumsy in my hands. The three-link coupling chain was stiff. 'Get it swinging,' advised Harry. I swung it back and forth, worked up momentum and threw it over the draw-hook. Somehow this made such a tangle that Harry had to free the three components by hand. Then I began to get the idea.

'Good,' said Harry, 'now we must get along. I want these four opens down in the shed. We'll push three away together. Once they get moving they'll roll. Then you go down to the shed, I'll start the last one off and you can practise coupling a moving wagon to a train.' Harry put his shunting pole between a wagon's wheel and the rail and levered upwards while I heaved against a buffer. The short raft of wagons began to move. 'Shunting poles aren't meant for this sort of thing, mind,' warned Harry breathlessly, 'there's a pinch bar down in the goods shed specially for the job but it's almost too heavy to carry.' When the trucks were well under way on the down grade, he stopped levering and left me to walk them into the shed, calling after me. 'Don't be in a hurry to swing your pole – move fast when the buffers clash.'

As the wagons drew alongside the goods shed platform, I forced down a hand-brake lever with my shunting pole, stopped the raft, put the coupling link into the ferrule hook and watched Harry start the last wagon. It rumbled towards me, seven and a half tons at five miles an hour. I tried to judge its closing speed as it bore down on me, apparently gaining in size and speed with every second that passed. Now! I swung my pole upwards in a perfectly timed movement; it passed between the buffers just as they were about to crash; they closed on it like vicious jaws and wrenched it painfully from my tightly clenched fists.

My hands felt paralysed and I walked up and down for a while running them on the seat of my trousers, regaining enough feeling in them to pick the pole up off the floor as Harry walked up.

'Hurt yourself?'

'No, startled,' I said with a grin.

His upper lip curled a bit at that. 'Come on, you'll soon find the knack. We must go to the station.' We walked along the track, past the wagon that Oakley's had loaded with straw bales.

'It looks a bit top-heavy, Harry.' I was amazed. I had called him Harry! Without thinking about it. The affair with the pole seemed to have broken down some reserve between us.

'Ah! That would be a job for my Duchess. She could have pulled that lot up to the load gauge to see if it was within the limits for passing under bridges.'

'So that's what those steel arches are for in sidings everywhere.'

'That's right – and talking of puzzles, have you found out what train carried twenty rear lamps?'

'You remember that? It must be five years since you asked me that. No I haven't asked anyone who hasn't been puzzled by it. What train was it?'

'Oho! I'm not telling you. You ought to know.' He seemed really pleased now and I relaxed. I felt that perhaps I was going to enjoy the job after all.

After filling in a big form to record wagon movements, Harry phoned Control to inform them and to order the extra wagons. While he was doing this, I asked Mr Halford if he knew about the train with twenty rear lamps but he only said, 'If it was anyone other than Harry, I'd say you were having your leg pulled.' The 10.30 stopper came and went and having attended to it we went back to the yard. 'We must sheet and rope that straw,' said Harry.

We walked at a pace that I was coming to recognise belonged to men long in railway service – a long striding, easy pace as if we were in a procession – passed the wagon of straw and entered the goods shed. Here Harry removed his jacket, put on a brown canvas apron that covered him from chest to ankles and rolled up his sleeves. In the corner were some folded tarpaulins. 'Pick up one of these sheets', he said, swinging one neatly turned bundle onto his shoulder, 'and bring it to the wagon.' I tried to pick it up and nearly overbalanced – they weighed about 56 pounds and were very clumsy.

Harry stood on the yard level and threw his 56 pounds seven feet to the top of the load, climbed up, unfolded the sheet to cover half the load and asked me to throw my sheet up to him. This was the moment of truth! After several attempts, he managed to catch the bundle, unfolded it and covered the other half of the load. Together we tied the sheets onto the cleats provided around the truck using string like heavily creosoted baler twine; then, with half-inch ropes we made the load quite secure. We stood back to admire our handiwork: a neatly folded black parcel on wheels.

'That's the way to do it, Adrian,' called a voice from the signal box opposite. I looked round to see Ken Rowlands leaning from the window.

'Hello, Ken.'

'Lovely job, Harry,' enthused Ken.

'Hello, Ken,' said Harry non-committally and then to me, 'Now this wagon'll be going "downhill" – to Weymouth, for Jersey – so I've laid the west end sheet overlapping the trailing east end sheet. If I hadn't, the slip-stream would get under the edge and soon it'd be billowing out like a sail even if it didn't blow off altogether.' I registered that little bit of expertise with great appreciation.

The wagon had then to be labelled and waybills made out before we retired to the station for tea and to wait for the Down stopper. As we walked past the sheeted wagon, I said to Harry, 'Goosey Dock is a funny name for a siding. Do you know how it got the name?'

'Well, it was built to take three coal wagons. As I've told you, the coal used to be drawn up in two ranks and they had to put a plank across from the outer to the inner wagon and bring it across the gap and through the other wagon to the horse and cart. So when they built the new station, they made the dock for the benefit of Toomer's and Langford's agents and as they both lived in Goosey … there you are. Good lord, back around 1930 they used to bring coal around the station cottages in the wheelbarrow for sale at 1s 10d a hundredweight. You think of that.'

At the station he asked me if I could read a timetable and when I said I could he set me problems: a morning train to Dolgelly, an afternoon train to Margate. In 1960 you could have gone to both those places from Challow in a day or half a day. When it was clear I knew what to do, he shut the book and said, 'Train times here haven't altered much in thirty-five years, there's fewer trains but them that are left are running at about the same times they did in 1924. The greatest change is having the 8.58 fast to London. That only came on about 1953 but then it was a bit late, leaving here at 9.20.'

'What were the other trains, Harry? You've told me about Sundays but what about week-days.'

'Ha! Ha! I think I shall surprise you. I think I'm right in saying that we had twenty-five trains in all, fourteen stoppers, the rest milk and goods – now we've got fourteen of all kinds, ten of them passengers.'

Mr Halford came out of his office and joined us. 'What were the other trains, Harry?'

'There were the empty and loaded milks, morning and evening. One empty, the Ladbroke Grove, got here at four in the morning. We had *five* Flys including one that got here at about 3.30 in the afternoon and left from here at 6. They called it the "Challow Goods".'

Mr Halford and I whistled and Harry was gratified by our astonishment and saw the question coming. 'We used to have a cattle and farm machinery market in the station yard every Monday; the sidings were packed with cattle trucks and empty opens for that. Then we had the Corn Store where all the local farmers came to collect their stocks of animal feeding stuff. There was the regular traffic in machinery from Nalder's at East Challow and from other works at Stanford and even Faringdon sometimes.' He broke off there as Ken 'rang the stopper in'.

We saw two passengers onto the 11.30 to Swindon and took the ticket from a man who got off. The train left, behind its ex-works engine, within a minute of arriving and we walked back across the footbridge. 'What else did you do here, Harry?'

'Well, keeping to regular traffic, we had the Station Truck twice a day. That used to come down from Paddington every morning with chocolates, cigarettes and butter and went back each night on a main line goods that stopped specially for it. Ha! You'll laugh when I tell you – Ody, the horse and cow slaughterer, used to send up the day's supply of corpses to Paddington in it.'

I think I must have worn him out with questions, making him talk more than he usually did, because when we got into the office he gave me a job. 'You can whitewash the edge of the platform. I'll show you where the stuff is.' He took me to the storeroom and in minutes I felt as if I was back in the Army; with a bucket of whitewash and an L-shaped brush I started to paint the edge of the 720-foot-long platform.

After twenty minutes I was rescued by the arrival of a lorry.

Harry came out, 'Put all that away and come to the goods shed, W & G's are here.' When I got to the shed Harry and the lorry driver were manhandling what looked like a miniature Nissen hut made of plywood from the lorry to the platform.

The lorry man was slim and small, about forty with a bald, egg-shaped head, a very wrinkled forehead and a ring of ragged, silver hair which hung round his neck as if it had slipped off the shiny, smooth cranium. 'Here's your mate come, Harry,' said he. 'Hey come on, kid, give us a hand here!'

The combined efforts of the three of us soon cleared the lorry, papers were handed over and the egghead driver climbed in and drove away. 'You'll have to learn how to shift these things on your own. They weigh about three hundredweight so you have to lever them across the floor with a pinch bar to get them under the crane – as there's two of us we can just slide them. Now get a piece of rope, tie it exactly round the middle of the pig-house and then bring the hook of the crane down to engage it.'

The travelling crane was an arrangement of chains and a lifting hook working through a box of gears suspended from a steel girder spanning the width of the shed. To lower the hook I pulled a cord and drew down the hook, and when I had slipped it under, the rope began to pull on the chain to wind the gears round; it was rather like winding up a very low-geared grandfather clock. When the pig-house was raised sufficiently to pass over the side of the truck, we pushed against the house and the box of gears rolled along the steel joist; when the pig-house was positioned over the wagon, I pulled the cord and down came the hook, settling the plywood pig-house into the wagon. Two could be fitted into each truck and the loaded vehicle was then pushed out of the shed, down the grade to bring the next truck under the crane.

There was the usual paperwork and labelling and as Harry was doing this, the 3-1 bell sounded for the Up stopper. 'Now there's a train that has run in its times since 1924 at least,' said Harry. 'Always around 12.25 here and every Monday for years it's had the stores van on the end. Yes – I know,' he smiled, 'what's the stores van? It brings all the clean washing round and takes away the dirty stuff and it also doles out soap, electric light bulbs and floor polish. There are several of them. They work from Swindon all over the place, every day of the week. You can order shunting poles – anything – from the General Stores down by the engine shed and next Monday up it comes in the stores van.'

The train arrived and was even more remarkable than Harry had described. It was hauled by an ex-works 'King' in gleaming, dark-green paint set off with plenty of brass and copper and by black bands and orange lines around the boiler and her three coaches were ex-Great Western stock; the first two were 1946 vintage but the stores van I recognised from a photograph as having once been part of Queen Victoria's Royal train of 1897 – a very handsome coach, panelled and carrying a clerestory roof. Harry exchanged the washing while I sat on the platform bench and admired the train and its engine, revelling in the comfortable fact that something like this train, at this time of day, had arrived at Challow each Monday morning for at least the last thirty-five years.

I thought I might be allowed to take the clean dusters to the signal box after the train had gone but I was handed a hoe and a rake and told to get busy on the weeds in the wide gravel strip between the fence and the platform paving. Harry went to the box.

It was an easy, pleasant job indeed, I began to think how nice it would be to have all the weeds cleared and the gravel smoothed straight. I looked at my recent effort at whitewashing – yes, that, too, looked smart and was asking to be completed. The Up platform was important because the nobs spent a fair length of time on it before catching their train whereas the Down platform they took little notice of as they hurried away to their cars at the end of the day. First things first. I would get the Up platform looking really smart; I began to feel proprietorial about Challow. I would make it a flower garden.

Harry let me off, hungry, at one o'clock. All the way home I was excited about the idea I'd had and the new feeling that was stealing over me concerning the station. I got indoors to find my mother waiting with a huge roast dinner; there would be no danger of my refusing it. I was ravenous.

'I've kept it hot but kept the gravy separate so it wouldn't dry up,' she said proudly.

'Thanks very much, Mum. I'll eat it all.'

'Well, how did you get on?' she stood over me eagerly, holding a saucepan.

'It was like the weather – it got better through the morning. Half the time I spent hoeing.'

'Hoeing?!' she said incredulously.

'Yes, it was really good. Are there any flower plants or seeds that I could put in now that would bloom this year?'

'Yes, we've got plenty in the greenhouse, coming on, but what sort of railway work did you do with Mr Strong?'

I told her but my mind was full of flowers.

Chapter Seven

Goosey and Gardening

There was no Fly to shunt and fewer parcels to book in next day, so that, after the 8.15 stopper Down, Harry and I were in the parcels office with nothing in particular to do for half an hour, so I took the opportunity to ask Harry where the station's garden had been before the place was rebuilt.

'Up against the wall of the road bridge on this side. It was a rockery. We were all keen gardeners then and we made a good job of it – even if I say so myself. Now you come to mention it, I think there's a photograph of it in the station master's office. I'll go and find it.'

He returned with a postcard print showing the Up platform ending against the west wall of the road bridge. Close to the wall, jutting up from the paving, was a timber 'bracket' signal carrying an arm for 'up the main' and a lesser arm on a left-hand bracket for 'up the loop'; immediately behind the signal the red-brick wall was painted white to provide drivers with better 'sighting' of the red arms. A bank of earth rose from the platform up the side of the bridge and on this was the station's garden. Annual flowers and herbaceous borders filled and surrounded a mnemonic of white-painted stones which extended from the top to the bottom of the bank, including, cleverly, the handsome signal in a display.

> Cornwall
> Has
> Attractive
> Landscapes
> Looe &
> Other
> Watering places
>
> Go Western Route

It was very well done – like something you might see in a winter garden at a seaside resort – I thought I could see Harry's precise care in every stone.

'It's marvellous, you must have taken a long time to put it together – it looks as if you found time to keep it tidy even when you had all those trains to see to.'

'It was about twenty feet from top to bottom. There wasn't anything like it for miles that I knew of. It was here when I came but we all kept it up. You only had to put a few minutes in after you'd booked off. Once or twice I came up for an hour on a Sunday afternoon, that's all.'

'You must like gardening. Do you do much at home?' Harry gave a short laugh and smiled momentarily. 'Ah! A bit. If you're passing through Stanford you could give me a call. You know where I live.' I said I did not know.

'Cottage on the bend – on the left after the Horse & Jockey. You can't miss it.'

I was quite keen on gardens too. Tidy, well-laid-out gardens arranged and tended by someone else were my favourite kinds though in the case of Challow I was keen to make a small garden – so I took him up on the offer. If his home garden was anything like the old station garden, it would be worth seeing.

'But what happened to the station garden here? There's no trace of it now.'

'It was dug up when the station was rebuilt before the war,' he said quietly, the pain he had felt then still in his voice and the way he emphasised 'dug'.

'Dug up?!'

'Well, they had to extend the platforms beyond the brick arch and put two tracks in on the down-side. So they took the old bridge away and put up the steel one out there. Then they dug foundations for this station – you've never seen such a mess. The old station was about fifty yards nearer the goods shed than this one.'

'But why didn't you make another garden?'

'I don't know really; we just didn't. That rockery had been put there by the old chaps when things were more settled. The old station was all wood, you know, just like Steventon now. I wouldn't be surprised if someone told me it was the original station from Brunel's time. It was comfortable, like an old armchair. Box was too – small, homely, without a lot of windows. There was an open fire in the back wall, raised off the floor with a side-oven so they could cook their meals when they were on twelve-hour shifts. The new signal box was raw concrete, you could've put the old box in that one's locking room, the new station was red brick. Looking back on it, it could've done with a garden to hide the rough edges but then it didn't seem much of a place for flowers.'

'What about putting a garden in now?' Harry looked sceptical. 'It could go along under the windows. There's a strip of gravel at the moment, about eighteen inches wide. That must have been designed to take a row of flowers ...'

Harry got down quickly from the high stool and went onto the platform saying, 'You're right, it never occurred to me.' I joined him outside and he continued, 'Dig the gravel out, go down a foot, fill it with top soil and you could have a lovely display – pack it with bulbs, annuals – wallflowers at the back, forget-me-nots at the front, we'd have a show from spring to autumn. I'll bring some plants from home.'

'My parents are going to bring some too,' I said.

'Well, that's good,' enthused Harry, 'the flowers'll be all round the platform seats – and you can do it all – it'll be *your* garden.' He felt he was being very generous, I think, and I wondered what was happening to me to make me happy at the prospect of gardening.

The passengers for the Cheltenham were arriving by then so we broke off to join in the ritual. After the train had gone Harry told Mr Halford what I proposed, received his blessing and then sat in the office planning what to plant for the best and longest show next year. We were interrupted by a knock on the door which then opened to admit a tall, stout, red-faced, hearty man.

'Morning, Harry!' he said in that curiously enthusiastic military voice I knew so well, and then, seeing me, 'Hello! Hearing about the old times, eh?'

'Not exactly, Mr Nelson,' said Harry. 'This is Adrian, our learner.'

'Oh! Well done!' cried Mr Nelson, advancing on me, beaming, his hand outstretched. We shook hands. 'I'm Tom Nelson, pleased to meet you!'

'I'm afraid we haven't got a wagon for your trailer, Mr Nelson – I suppose you've brought one?' said Harry, in a 'let's get to the point' sort of voice. 'I've got one on order.'

'Oh blast! That means it'll arrive on Wednesday and the trailer won't go out till Friday. Damn shame – not the way the old Great Western would have done things, eh?!' He spoke in a tone of enthusiastic resignation – rumbling cheerfully – not at Harry but at 'the Railway'. Harry seemed to understand this. 'Yes, we used to fight the roads once, but that was a long time ago. Where's the trailer going?'

'Oh! Somewhere in Shropshire. If it was closer I'd take it there meself. I've had them on the phone. Their old trailer has had it so they've treated themselves to one of mine but they need it *now*.'

'Well then, there's no worry. The Up Fly'll bring the "Flat" tomorrow and they can wait while we load it, then it'll be taken to Didcot for Oxford and the north. I'll get on the phone to Didcot yard and make sure they send it on smartly.'

'Well done, Harry! That sounds first class. Do come round for a drink one day, won't you?' Mr Nelson turned to me, 'I've asked him often enough but he never comes. Well, good luck, I'll go up and see Ken in the box and then go home!' He crashed the platform side-door open and shut and thundered off along the platform.

'Who was that?' I asked in amazement as the dust stirred up by his departure settled. 'He sounded like every old Colonel I've ever met all rolled into one.'

'That was Commander Tom Nelson – retired Navy man. They say he had a destroyer during the war. He's got a farm out Kingstone Lisle way and makes these trailers. He's mad on the old Company. You'd like to talk to him.'

'My God! I can just imagine him on the bridge of a destroyer doing thirty knots through an Atlantic storm and asking them to go faster. What a bloke!'

Harry grinned a moment. 'Yes, he does strike you a bit like that when you first meet him. He's a very decent sort. Let's go and take his trailer off the car.'

We walked down to Goosey Dock where a very fine 1947 Jaguar was standing.

'My goodness, Harry, what a lovely car!'

'Yes, he's an expert on them, got quite a collection so they say.'

GWR wages grade staff at Challow in 1924. From the left: Tom Gillman, Harry Strong, Harry Crooks, who was killed on the line, Reg Chester – possibly a guard – and ? Reynolds. GWR caps were taller than BR-issued caps but the blue serge three-piece suits were very similar to the BR suit I was issued with – and, of course, the character of the men was the same in 1924 as 1960. (Courtesy the late Harry Strong/Author's collection)

Some of the staff at Challow station in 1946. Albert Stanley, Bessie Perry and Sam Loder's wife, Dorothy, who was 'Ayres' before she married Sam. She was Auntie to Pam Ayres. The lorry driver – face cut off in the camera – was Ken Rowlands. (Michael Stanley/Author's Collection)

The Bristol–Swindon and Swindon–Didcot route was blessed with a regular daily service of 'all stations' trains hauled by passenger engines just out of the Works. They had a week of 'running-in' and, sometimes, the following week we got an even bigger thrill – that of seeing the engine that had been footling with two coaches come thundering through at 70 mph with twelve on. No. 7007 *Great Western* was turned out of Swindon Works new in July 1946 and was then named *Ogmore Castle*. In January 1948, at Nationalisation, it was renamed *Great Western*. The name had the obvious significance of commemorating the noble old Company but that was also the name of the first express engine to be built at Swindon in 1846. Seen here at Challow in September 1960 on the 10.45 Didcot–Swindon 'stopper', No. 7007 has just had its last general repair and is 'running in'. The engine was scrapped in February 1963 having run, on average, 51,615 miles a year since new. A very new recruit to BR(WR), nineteen-year-old porter Adrian, is just visible on the right – looking on, besotted. (H. O. Vaughan)

The pleasure of working for the coal-fired railway was a mixture of the splendid characters one worked with – human and machine. One worked surrounded by things that appeared right and proper. (H. O. Vaughan/Author's Collection)

'Where's the trailer? I can't see it.'

'Aha! You will when you get round behind the car.' Attached to the back of the car was the most unusual – and sensible – trailer I had seen. It was 20 feet long and 3 inches off the ground, you could easily toss bales onto it 'ten high'.

'It's his own idea,' said Harry. 'He's got the patent for it. Come on, let's uncouple it and stand it ready by the Dock. Then we'll go up the box, get the details off Nelson and do the wagon labels and as much paperwork as we can – everything but the wagon number in fact.'

We went over to the signal box. Mr Nelson was sitting in the armchair drinking tea. 'Have a cup?' Ken asked Harry and me, not really waiting for an answer but pouring it out. A block bell rang and I looked at Ken. 'Go on then,' he said, throwing me the duster.

'Aha! Keen man,' chuckled Mr Nelson. 'Is everyone that works on the railway an enthusiast?'

'I think railway work is pleasant – you come along and enjoy your shift, your own boss, out in the country. Though I can't say I like night shift.' That was Ken.

'It depends what you're doing. I had a job – I still have it but I've got my motorbike now – I used to leave home at midnight and cycle ten miles to Steventon, get there just before two and open the station to let GPO men take mail bags off the Up Postal. Five minutes, they'd have gone, I'd lock the shop up and come home. But that was the job, you did it and never thought if it was hard. Only now I've got my popper do I think back at all the heavy cycling I did.' That was Harry.

'But you never worried, did you?' said I. 'Or you wouldn't have cycled here on a Sunday to see to the garden.'

'Of course not. When things are easier you look back and wonder how you managed before. We took the rough with the smooth and were just as happy then as now.'

'Happier probably,' I said, 'because you had your old station with a lovely garden.'

'You used to come up here in your spare time to look after the station's garden, Harry?' asked Mr Nelson. Bells rang, I answered them and pulled off down the main. Harry had not spoken, so I said, 'I don't think railwaymen were "enthusiasts" in the sense you mean. The atmosphere of the railway must have been like the spirit in the Army – the CO set the pace and each man's keenness grew into a competition to be as smart or smarter than the next man, each platoon tried to be better at weapon training or whatever than the next lot.'

'It was called "morale",' broke in Mr Nelson in another voice, quiet and serious. 'I think you are right. The railway used to be very busy and there were a lot more men employed. The men had to be pretty good at their job or else get washed away in the flood of work. Busy men, working together, make for good morale and the spirit is passed on over the years. You were in the Army, Adrian?' I said I was. 'Then you'd understand. That is how it was in the Navy. We were proud of our ship but we didn't think of ourselves as enthusiasts – we left that to the land-lubbers. Oh! Look at this!'

His voice went back to its enthusiastic tone and we turned to look where he'd pointed just as a polished 'Castle' burst under the steel span and came thumping heavily past the box at something close to 70 mph. I counted eight Pullman cars behind her.

'My God, those chaps were going well! Did you see the name of the engine, Adrian?' asked Nelson.

'*Earl of Clancarty*,' I replied happily, putting the signal levers back.

'Those Pullman coaches look good behind a "Castle" – that was the South Wales Pullman, I suppose.'

'Yes – 8.50 Paddington,' said Ken, 'she's five minutes down but at that rate they'll be "right time" Swindon.'

I thought we were all set for a pleasant hour watching trains but Harry had finished his tea and was going to show me the Great Western way, which was not, as Mr Nelson had said, hanging about behind a teacup. He took the necessary details about the trailer from Mr Nelson then took me from the box.

In the goods shed I filled in the wagon labels and watched him make out the waybills in his fine, flowing handwriting. We then went for what he called 'a poke around' and looked into every nook and cranny in the shed; just looking, counting piles of folded tarpaulins, lifting lids off old oil-drums, followed by a stroll through the yard, past the shovelling coalmen right to the very buffers of the siding. Only then did he turn back and return to the station to wait for the Up stopper.

This came and went, picking up two passengers and putting off a parcel for a local garage. Harry phoned the trader, told me to enter details in the ledger and then said, 'Do you think you could learn about station accountancy?' He might as well have asked if I'd like an ice-cold shower.

'I shouldn't think I could at all.'

'Oh dear, why not?'

'Books of figures don't ever work for me.'

'Well, you'll have to learn how to sell tickets and book them in properly afterwards. When you take charge here, you'll have to look after the booking office for four trains. Come on, I'll take you into the office.'

We went in and he told Basil what had to be done. I thought Basil would show me, as he was the booking clerk. Instead, he stood to one side while Harry got the various ledgers down and began to explain them and the rack full of tickets; in a drawer there were Great Western Railway season tickets, decorated like a one pound note and nearly as big. Harry was obviously as much at home in this clerkish place as in Goosey Dock sheeting a wagon, but I have a mental block where paperwork is concerned and stood at his side despairing of ever understanding it all. Indeed, I was almost asleep on my feet – Harry had not even noticed, so keen was he on the system he was explaining – when the telephone rang and Basil answered it. His eyes lit up. He looked round at me and said, 'Thanks Ken, I'll tell them all.'

'That was Ken to say that the 8.45 Padd has failed at Didcot. It's off Steventon now and' – he paused for a climax – '*City of Truro* is bringing it down.' I was so excited I rushed out onto the platform quite unconcerned at breaking off my lesson with Harry. The point was that the 8.45 was the Bristolian and, doubly

Having done its duty and rescued the passengers of the highly prestigious Bristolian from a dismally failed diesel, No. 3440 *City of Truro* made its way back to Didcot in the afternoon. It was 'put in for a Fast' at Challow and then 'turned out main line' to run home to Didcot. The signal Up platform line to Up main can be seen lowered above the engine's boiler. This must have been one of the gallant engine's last duties before it was returned to the National Railway Museum at Clapham. (H. O. Vaughan)

important, it was now being hauled by a small (by modern standards) 'four-coupled' engine built in 1903 which had been in a museum from 1931 to 1957. Mr Halford, Basil and Harry joined me on the platform, all of us looking forward to a thrilling show. *City of Truro* was the first engine in the world to reach 100 mph, which she did when she was new, hauling an 'Ocean Mail Special' in 1904. The men at Didcot, where she was shedded, came in on their days off to make sure she was in perfect working order and even drivers spent time helping to keep her spotlessly clean. One of these men had said to me, 'We think the world of her. She'll steam on a candle flame; it doesn't matter how you fire her – "haycock", "saucer", "flat" or "all up in the corner" – she'll always be "on the mark".'

And now this fifty-seven-year-old paragon was standing in for a twelve-month-old diesel. I watched her racing towards me down the long straight from Wantage Road – a tall, narrow little engine, the Bristolian headboard on her smokebox, designed for the fat boiler of a 'Castle' and several sizes too big for her. She was running very upright, so it seemed, with no rocking or swaying – she was all *pull*. Her outside cranks caught the sun each time they turned over, which was very rapidly, so that I saw a constant twinkling of bright steel and, as she drew closer, the silver blur of her coupling rod against the dark red of her frames.

Clear as a flute her whistle sounded as she approached our group. We glimpsed her driver, hand on brake handle, head thrust forward to the look-out window; we saw her fireman in the act of shooting another shovelful into her furnace and she was through, that 1903 museum piece, at something like 80 mph. Her crew, lately off the diesel, were obviously delighted to have her and were showing their respect for her capabilities by driving her harder, in all probability, than she had ever been driven before. They knew *she* would not fail them. This realisation together with the noble sight and sound she made brought a lump to my throat. From that moment I despised diesel locomotives with an intensity that would take years to subside.

I needed several cubic yards of top soil for my garden, and next day, as much to find an excuse to speak to them as to find the soil, I asked the three girls who caught the 8.15 stopper to Swindon where such quantities of loam might be obtained. Much to my surprise the red-haired girl said, 'There's enough soil and compost lying around our place for a hundred gardens – our Dad won't mind. Come round on Saturday and get some. But what are you going at?' I told her the plan and they were all very pleased, each suggesting flowers that would look nice and so we talked till the train came. I ushered them on and it steamed away – then I realised I did not know who the red-haired girl was. Harry did. 'Her name's Veronica. She lives at the farm on your road home.'

The parcels lorry came and went, day by day; the Fly shunted; and I began to improve in the use of the pole; tickets remained a blank. On Friday I was introduced to another piece of ritual: the Winding of the Clock. This was the public time-piece which hung on the wall facing the platform, high up, under the platform canopy. Just before eleven o'clock Harry took a chair and a special clock-winding crank and went out onto the platform. He knocked on a window and Basil opened it as he climbed onto his chair, opened the clock's glass front and wound the spring. Basil was standing by the phone to the signal box, the instrument in his hand, listening.

'Time! Time! Time!' he called. Harry pushed the minute hand forward by thirty seconds, closed the case and stepped down. It was nothing really but he so gave his mind to whatever he was doing that it seemed to be important – everything to do with the railway was important to him. He was the personification of the old rhyme 'for the want of a nail the battle was lost' and made sure that all nails in his care were firmly driven home.

Saturday came – a weekend off – and I drove down to the station around eleven o'clock. Harry helped me move the platform seats out of the way; I took a four-wheel barrow for the spoil and began digging the gravel out to make way for topsoil, each piled barrow being tugged to the east end of the platform and the contents dumped in the grass. By one o'clock I had cleared the whole length under the windows and went over to the Prince to have a pie and a pint. Just as I was finishing Basil came in so I had another.

'What do you think of it all then?' he asked.

'Well, it's all right – the more active parts of a porter's life are interesting.'

'You mean you can't do the booking side of it?'

'Well, I meant what I said but I dare say one of the reasons why I can't do the accountancy part is because I find it incredibly boring.'

'Huh! I don't mind it at all. You'd better learn about it before you "take on", I don't want my ledgers messed up every evening so that I've got to clear up behind you.'

'Well, I'll never be able to do it – I can manage the goods paperwork though.'

'Harry can do it all – he ought to have been a station master at some big station. He read *Rules and Regulations for Station Accountancy* like you or I would read Hank Janson. I've seen him sitting with his coffee in one hand and that great thick book in the other. Even station masters ask him for advice. He's red hot on signalling rules too – he was a signalman once.'

'Yes, I know. He is amazing. He must be very contented with being a porter not to have taken promotion over all the years he's been on. It's obvious he could have had it if he wanted – you only have to apply when a vacancy comes up.'

'Yeah – no ambition,' said Basil sadly, looking at his empty glass.

'Come on, drink up. I'll buy *you* one.'

'No, no thanks. I've had two now. I'd better get on. I'll see you on Monday. Cheerio.'

I tied the four-wheel barrow to the car's rear bumper and drove round to the farm in second gear. Veronica was pleased to see me and her father came over for a look.

Tom Carter was a short man who looked immensely powerful. He had a cheerful farmer's face on a stocky neck, his fair hair was tousled, bursting out in all directions from beneath a cloth cap set awry towards the back of his head. His jacket was green, tweedy and stuck with bits of straw from the job he had just left. His trousers were of cavalry twill once cream; his boots, crunching and squelching through the farmyard muck, were massive.

'Hey-up!' he roared hospitably, 'so you're the gardener. When V'ronica told me I said I'd come round wi' the tractor and trailer and bring a load – but seeing how well you're provided for –' he swept an arm in the direction of my Morris with a platform barrow tied to her tail – 'I'll let you get on with it. Help yourself!' He went off chuckling with sarcasm before I could say anything in reply. Veronica 'helped me to load the barrow, I set off to the station and threw my haul into the hole. The great pile on the barrow turned into a little pile in the trench and I saw that the job was going to take all afternoon – quite a pleasant prospect, in fact.

Returning to the farm I discovered that Veronica had an elder sister, Jenny – about my age – who was very blonde, very pretty and as slim as her father was stocky. Returning for the fourth time I was met by the girls' mother who had tea and home-made cake waiting. By the end of the afternoon I had made a lasting friendship with the Carter family which made the main object of the day's effort – to prepare a flower bed – seem of secondary importance. But all was now ready; in such conditions flowers would blossom magnificently.

Chapter Eight

Sam Entertains

I drove into a football match when I arrived at the station on Monday. In the car park Basil and Sam were opposing two men I had not seen before, both wearing bib-and-brace overalls. They were well matched. Sam and the older, overalled man both tall and roughly the same age; Basil and the other man, young and fit. They were all making a lot of noise and I wondered what Harry was thinking about it. As I parked and got out of the car they stopped playing, came over and stood around me and the car.

'Hi-up, Ady – you're early,' said Sam.

'It's nearly two o'clock.'

'That's early when you're learning – half past would do and then you wouldn't have missed anything.'

'Harry's got him trained,' said the young man in overalls.

'No – that's his military punctuality,' said the older man, and together they rocked the Morris from side to side. 'Nice little bus – got good springs, Maurice.'

'Not half – just what I could do with, John.'

'Get off, you silly beggars. I'm here because it's two and that's my time.'

'He's here because he's here because he's here because he's here!' the older man began to the tune of 'Auld Lang Syne' and was immediately followed by the other three. I began to feel very hot – someone ought to get his nose punched at this stage, I thought, looked round angrily for a victim, saw that they were all at least as big as I and decided against it.

They stopped singing with a kind of whoop and Sam said, nodding towards the overalled pair, 'That's John Moody and his little mate Maurice Sworn. Haven't you met them before?'

'I think I might have seen them on the track last week but I didn't take a lot of notice.'

'You'll take more notice in future,' they said, each jumping on a running board of my car and swaying it while they sang 'Life on the Ocean Wave'.

'Who are they, Sam?' I had to shout above the row. They stopped singing and swaying and stood, breathless on the car, grinning hard, looking at Sam and me. Sam said, looking straight at them, 'They're the Signal and Telegraph department linemen – an idle lot of scivers who drink tea in every hut, house and signal box from here to Steventon.'

The linemen jumped off the car. 'Gettim, Maurice!' They advanced on Sam in the stance of all-in wrestlers. 'Up Guards and at 'em!' shouted Basil. Sam backed away as John and Maurice advanced. I saw where it was leading, they were herding him backwards to a lock-up garage whose door was wide open. Sam's heel caught the projecting 'stop' for the door, he tripped and fell. In an instant the door was closed on him. A great cheer went up outside while from within a hollow voice boomed, 'Come on, let me out. I've got things to do.'

'What's Sammy got to do then?' they teased him with imitations of his pleadings. I was only amazed that they had the nerve to riot within feet of Harry's door and went in to sign on.

I expected to find a very stern-looking Harry – but the room was empty. I put my head round the booking office door. No one there. He was not in the lavatory either. Perhaps he had gone down the yard to escape the noise and – as I thought – un-railwaymanlike behaviour. I was at a loss to know what to do because he had the keys; I could not even get a hoe from the store in order to clear some weeds.

Sam came in hitching up his trouser and straightening his tie. 'Mad lot they are, stopping people from working.' The football match had resumed.

'Where's Harry? Down in the yard?'

'No!' laughed Sam. 'He's on lates at Wantage Road covering the vacancy. Him and Albert are on the relief and, as it's a longish journey for both of them to Wantage, they take it in turns to go there. Albert did his late turn there last week and so he's doing his *early* turn here this week. He went over home just before you arrived – I relieved him at half past one.'

'But where's Mr Halford?'

'He's gone down to Uffington in his car – that's how that garage door was open – he's station master there too, you see. Come on over to the down-side; we'll wait for the stopper.'

We walked over the footbridge and sat down on a four-wheel barrow. The sun was warm on our backs and the air was quiet. 'Well, that explains all the racket – I couldn't understand how Harry allowed it.'

'Old Harry's a wet blanket,' said Sam, 'he's the best there is at his job but don't take him too seriously. Oh! Look at this,' pointing up the track, 'old Bill's pushing his luck. Here comes the Kensington past the stopper.'

Three quarters of a mile away, I could see a 'Castle' on the Down main, a great column of smoke billowing upwards as she accelerated hard past a '61' class tank engine drifting down the relief line on the Didcot to Swindon stopper. After a few seconds we caught the sound of her exhaust and saw a spurt of pure white steam rise from her whistle – steam rose from the tank engine's reply as they passed; there was a second's pause before the sound reached us.

The Kensington came roaring down to the station and burst through, the engine – 7020 *Gloucester Castle* – pulling for all she was worth. Her train of six-wheeled milk tanks drummed out their peculiarly exciting rhythm – dum-dum-dum, dum-dum-dum – rapidly. I wanted to jump up and cheer! She blew a grateful whistle to

Bill Mattingley for letting her through and roared into the distance, the beautiful exhaust music coming back on the wind.

'That's when it's good to see them,' said Sam enthusiastically. 'In the collar and working hard.'

'The driver wasn't half laying it on. Was that just because he'd been allowed past the stopper? They aren't usually so keen.'

'They're the men off the eight o'clock Cheltenham – they're going home! Ah, but there's more to it than that. When they get to Swindon they come off the tanks – another engine takes them down to Cardiff – and that "Castle" goes onto a fast for Gloucester. The stopper makes a connection with it at Swindon. So it's better for the "tanks" to go first so the engine can get onto the Gloucester train and be ready and waiting, rather than have to trail along behind the stopper all the way.'

The stopper ran in then and Sam went into his 'Challer' routine and took a couple of tickets. No one got on. The signal to leave the platform was lowered and the train drew slowly forward. As it drew level with the signal box, the signal to go out from the relief line to the main line was lowered – slowly – as a hint to the driver not to go rushing off. He took his train, drifting, down to the advanced starting signal, number 54, 700 yards further on. Sam and I watched the signal box.

'Ol' Bill's up on the frame waiting for the road,' murmured Sam. A minute passed, the stopper was close to 54 signal. Suddenly Bill's shadowy figure moved. We saw his hand thumping the bell tapper – even when he was not in a hurry he was inclined to be rough with the bells – then he strode quickly to the end of the frame and swung the lever over. I imagined I saw the box shake. 54 signal stabbed downwards, the '61' tooted acknowledgement and snorted off to Uffington.

The football match was over when we got back to the office and Basil was sitting at his desk, working on some papers. Sam went in and sat on the table, half covering the work. 'Hi-up, Bas. Got a lot to do?' Basil threw him off after a tussle which swept away a mass of papers onto the floor. I was amazed; after a week with Harry I had never seen anything even slightly indecorous happen, except perhaps that guard, and he was *quietly* drunk. These people did not even have the excuse of drunkenness: 'Come on Ady,' said Sam, 'let's go and clean the Tilleys; we aren't wanted here.'

'Is it always like this?' I asked, as we walked to the lamp hut at the end of the platform.

'Like what? Oh, larking around! 'Tis when we get a chance. But that's how the railway always was. You've only ever been with Harry. You can do your job without going round with a long face all day.'

'Harry's all right,' I said. 'He likes to be quiet, that's all.'

'Well, we like a joke now an' then. Look here, I'll show you how to service the Tilleys before you put them out. The glass needs cleaning on some of them, the wire inside the vaporising tube often needs decoking, and every now and then we have to put a new mantle on one.'

We worked away at this for a while. 'Sam, did you ever hear of a train with twenty rear lamps?'

'Huh! That's the sort of train we need – twenty lamps to clean, fill and trim.'

'Harry says he saw it every day when he first came on the railway.'

'Get away! Perhaps old Harry is having a joke for once. I wouldn't know, it would be long before my time. How could any train have twenty tail lamps?'

'I wonder if Albert knows?'

'Well, he started back in 1920 and was over at Patney, which wasn't far from Harry's place so perhaps he might –' At that moment there was a terrific crash on the roof of the iron hut and the interior boomed like a drum. 'That's that Basil!' roared Sam, charging out of the shed. I followed, my heart still pounding from the fright.

Basil was running along the track side towards the signal box, looking back to see if Sam was chasing him, when he passed 56 signal, the arm of which was lowered and now swung up to 'Danger'. There was an almighty bang and Basil, off balance, fell over like a startled rabbit. He had fallen perfectly into Bill's favourite ambush – an explosive fog signal placed on the signal arm's cast-iron 'stop'. Bill stood at the signal box window giving the boxer's salute as Basil picked himself up off the gravel. 'Come on, Ady,' called Sam to me, 'tea break.'

After tea we left the box, heading, I thought, for the station.

'Answer the phone for us, Bas,' asked Sam.

'Why, where are you going?' said Basil suspiciously, for with the sort of feud those two had going they could never be sure of even innocent actions.

'We'll be on the down-side, waiting for the watercress. Ady, bring the ledger labels and the outwards book over, will you?'

After a quarter of an hour, a small, green van arrived and out of it we took four dozen 'chips' of cress, each weighing about four pounds. We sorted them onto two four-wheel barrows – the 'uphills' and the 'downhills' – the latter to go away on the parcels train due at 4 p.m. and the others to go out on the 4.30 passenger train. Sam, always alert, bought some chips at 1s 6d each to sell to the crews of goods trains that stopped at the station on the Down relief line, his first customers being the men on the parcels train.

With the Down line watercress away behind a 'Hall' class engine we pulled the other barrow across to the Up platform to await the 4.30 Up train. This had good connections at Didcot for the north and north-west and was fast from Didcot to London, so there was always a handful of passengers. The usual quota had arrived and were standing on the platform, staring idly along the line or looking down at the rails. One man was standing about ten feet from our office door, his back towards us. 'Watch this now,' commanded Sam. I looked through the window, wondering if Sam was going to shove him under a train.

Sam approached the man silently from the rear and, just as he was passing, gave a quick burst of 'How's-yer-bum?' loud and sudden. The victim, startled out of his reverie by a deep voice in his ear, whirled round to see who had spoken, but of course there was no one in sight. Sam turned sharply and was walking back towards the office as the dazed man turned back to face the rails. 'Nice bit of sun,' said Sam with a cheerful nod as he strolled past. He came back to the office, his face red and twitching with suppressed laughter. 'How was that?'

'A cunning stunt – as we used to say in the Army – where did you get that from, the Marx brothers? I think you've stunned *him*; look he's sort of staggering off up the platform. T'isn't the way to encourage passengers though, is it?'

'Ah – go on, you enjoyed it.'

'I did, but I could live without it. Look out, here comes the stopper. We'll get that cress on now.'

'Hang on, wait for me, you're too eager.' We tumbled out onto the platform.

The three girls from the 8.15 Down in the morning got off the train. Veronica walked home, the other girl got into a car that was waiting for her and the youngest came to ask for the lock-up to be opened so she could take her bicycle out. Sam obliged her and wheeled the bike out – with its saddle back to front.

'What rotten sod did this!' demanded Sam in a great sweat.

The twelve-year-old girl squeaked, 'Oh! My bicycle!'

'Don't you worry, love,' said Sam, consolingly, 'it can easily be mended – if we can find the right spanner, there should be one somewhere in Stanford.'

'Oh, you ... *Loder*!' She obviously knew all about Sam and had, I think, stronger language on the tip of her tongue. 'Just you put it back straight for me.'

Mr Halford must have heard the commotion, for he came out into the yard – or it might have been his teatime.

'What's the matter, Sam?'

'Er, nothing at all, Mr Halford. This young lady's bicycle fell over and twisted the saddle round. Isn't that right, dear?' She smiled sweet fury up at him, Sam turned the saddle, she put her satchel in the wicker basket on the front handlebars and cycled away. Sam walked back to the door of the office.

'Well, it must be about teatime. I'll be off,' said Mr Halford. Basil, hearing this, got up from his desk, grabbed his jacket off the hook and came out fast – tripped over Sam's nicely placed foot – and hurried away.

We put on our own kettle and settled down for some sandwiches and cake.

'I like that young girl with the bike,' said Sam, sitting back in a chair he'd brought from the booking office.

'You'd surprise her if you told her.'

'Ah! But did you see how she went for me? She didn't cry – or anything like it – she was just about to cuss blue flashes.'

'What if you'd made her cry?'

'I've seen her on and off trains for three years now. I know her too well for that. She's a fine girl.'

'The 5.5's the next on the Down,' Sam said, 'for Swindon, Chippenham, Bath and Bristol but on Fridays only there's no 5.5 and we have the 5.25 instead. Now that's for Newport and the south Wales main line, so if anyone comes here after a ticket for Chippenham on a Friday night – *remember* – and don't sell him one till the 5.25's gone. Somebody here forgot that once and sent a man for Chippenham all the way to Newport and he never got home till after midnight and his missus accusing him of all sorts of things. We had to give him a note for her in the end.'

After tea we went out to light our fourteen Tilley lamps and distributed them around the station in time for the passengers off the 5.50 Swindon to Didcot stopper. We carried a lamp in each hand, taking them to the lamp standards at the furthest end of the long platforms and to the top of each stairway of the footbridge. It was a tedious business even with two of us traipsing backwards and forwards, and I made a note to start the job in plenty of time when I came to do the job on my own. Darkness was closing in on the station by the time we had them all in position. The 5.50 Swindon arrived in the twilight and the 5.5 Paddington stopped at the station in darkness; the coaches' lights showing yellow; the big engine only a silhouette with a core of bright firelight.

When these trains had gone there was nothing to do until the 8.30 Up stopper. Sam put a few lumps of coal on the waiting room fire in case we should get a passenger or two. We adjourned to the station master's office where the chairs were more comfortable, the surroundings were cream coloured rather than dark brown, and the booking-office ticket window was within earshot.

'Do you think you'll like it here?' asked Sam, with his feet on the station master's desk.

'Yes, I'm sure I shall, but I don't know how I'll manage that ticket business, booking it all in afterwards.'

'Well, I'll show you, it's easy enough.' He swung his long legs off the desk, stood up and went over to the ticket-rack and the dreaded ledgers. I groaned inwardly but thought it would be better to try and take something in. Having it explained for a second time enabled me to memorise the salient points of the procedure and Sam finished, 'You've got it then?'

'Oh, yes thanks, Sam, very good of you, I'm sure I'll be able to manage. Shall we put the kettle on?' Sam agreed enthusiastically.

While it was boiling, a knock came on the ticket-window. 'In you go and see to that,' ordered Sam grimly. I went in and lifted the ticket-flap. A young man and woman were bowing from the waist, peering in at me.

'Two singles to Paddington, please.'

He spoke in a matter-of-fact voice with a strong London accent; he was confident that I would produce those things in a moment; he had no idea of the turmoil he had aroused within my breast but he might soon receive an inkling.

I searched for the tickets. It was very interesting to see the number of Great Western Railway tickets we had in stock – there was a 'Cheap Day' to Weymouth and another to Weston-super-Mare, green card with a red 'D'; I found a pink GWR ticket for dogs accompanying passengers; it seemed as if all our first-class tickets were white GWR card, and I made a note to buy some for souvenirs. Then I realised that I'd forgotten what the man had asked for.

'Er, um, sorry, what did you ask for?' I had expected him to be cross but I think he was too taken aback to be anything but puzzled.

'Two singles to London.'

I found them in the end – Western Region tickets – I punched them in the date stamp and was about to hand them over when I remembered that I had not charged him for them – and I did not know the fare or where I might find it. I felt my face go red; I felt clumsy and stupid – I *was* clumsy and stupid – and I *hated* the bloody job. I went to the door and looked in on Sam serenely pouring the tea, doubtless wondering whatever was taking me so long. 'Psst! Sam!' I whispered. 'What's the fare for a single to Padd?'

'Ten and sixpence,' he said laconically over his shoulder.

Feeling grateful and relieved I went back to the ticket-window to find that my customers had vanished. I bent down to the little oval hole in the glass. 'Hello! Anyone there?' The young man came out of the waiting room. 'Ah, here you are then,' I said, trying to be brisk and businesslike, 'that'll be a guinea please.'

'What's a guinea in English?'

'Well they're half a guinea each, you see, so that ...'

'Yeah, OK. But what's a half-guinea – in money.'

'Oh! I see, twenty-one shillings please,' I gave him a winning smile through the little glass window and he bowed down as he pushed the exact money through the oval hole. I just retained sufficient presence of mind to push the tickets through before I dropped the slide.

I went back to the parcels office feeling exhausted. 'Give me some tea quick – what's it all on that tray for? – my God, it's rough dealing with the public. That chap didn't even know what a guinea was. I'd rather be in the box than looking after crowds of passengers.'

'We're just going to give them some tea and biscuits,' said Sam, 'I always do that for any 8.30 passengers because the pot's usually full at this time. Come on, we'll go and chat them up.' There was no point in trying to argue with him. My cup was on the tray and in miserable embarrassment I followed Sam round to the waiting room.

Sam had an imposing figure when he drew himself up in a military way and in this manner he now swept elegantly through the doorway, the teatray supported delicately on the fingertips of his right hand; he brought it down with a flourish and landed it gently on the table. I sidled round the door behind him. 'Good evening, ladies and gentlemen' – I relaxed, at least he had not gone into his other routine – 'tea is served.'

I suppose if you come to a little country station in the middle of a dark, remote-seeming country, seventy miles from your home in London, and you are sold your tickets by a man who shows every symptom of being – at best – a halfwit and then, as you sit huddled over an open fire at the end of a long, cold, leather-covered horsehair sofa, a man over six feet tall steps in with all the elegance of an evil and mysterious butler and announced that tea you never asked for is now served, you could be forgiven for feeling nervous, for wondering if you had arrived at a railway station at all. They certainly looked nervous then, as Sam the Butler bent solicitously over them, handing out cups and asking how many lumps of sugar they required.

'Going home then?' asked Sam.

'Er, yes,' said the young man.

'Will the train be long?' asked his girl timidly.

'No, not long now. Been out for the day, have you?'

'Er – yes.'

'Looking round the old follies and churches and things?' Perhaps Sam's accent got through to them because the girl now relaxed a little.

'Yes, my people came from Faringdon long ago and we've had a day out and tried to find mention of them in the town.'

'Yeah, we even been rahnd the churchyard looking at the headstones. Give me the creeps it did, even in broad daylight.'

'Oh, Fred! It was nice – quiet and sunny.' She looked at Sam. 'We had some beer and a pasty sitting on the churchyard wall in the sun.' She seemed to be a very nice girl, I thought.

'Ah, but I wouldn't go round them places after dark,' said Sam, leaning forward in his seat. 'I've lived here all my life and I don't even like walking across the car park to my house in the dark.'

Oh Lord! Here we go, Loder's scared of the dark. I wondered what was coming next, or even if he knew himself.

'No because there's a haunted farm on one side of the road and there might be a ghost here too.' The girl slipped her arm around Fred's though he didn't look much like a protector from where I sat. The firelight flickered over their pale London faces.

'It was here that the first death took place on the Great Western Railway, one hundred and twenty years ago next month, when this station was the terminus of the line from Paddington. A train came down from London, the driver fell asleep at the controls and the train crashed into the buffers. He was killed.' He paused. 'They never found his fireman. Now, the old station was pulled down thirty years ago and they do say that since then the dead don't walk the line at nights and that the ghostly train don't come through on its anniversary but I –' *Whoooooooooo.* The girl screamed and buried her face in Fred's frozen shoulder; even Sam and I got a nasty fright as the fast blew its whistle passing through.

'Come on,' said Sam, 'have another cup of tea.' But when they did not answer, he said, 'Oh well, I'll call you when your train comes,' swept the tray up onto his fingertips and strode out of the room. I think even he realised he'd gone too far.

'You're a handy specimen,' I said when we got back to our office. 'You scared the wits out of them and you even gave me a fright when the whistle blew.'

'What d'you mean? I didn't know the train was coming and I didn't blow the whistle.'

'Still, it was a good story – how much of it is true?'

'Well, the bit about the crash is true – I read it in a book. I was only trying to give them a bit of atmosphere, just to pass the time.'

'I reckon they're stiff with your atmosphere; we'll probably have to carry them onto the stopper.' The stopper arrived shortly after and we put the couple onto it with great and even exaggerated politeness, as I realised when they had gone. 'I bet they thought we were taking the micky.'

'Trust you to look on the black side; no wonder you and Harry get on so well.'

'Ah! I'm sorry, Sam. I've had a good shift this afternoon.'

'Have you?' he said, brightening immediately. 'Well, get along home and I'll see you tomorrow.'

Chapter Nine

Albert's Railway

There was a rodeo at the station next day. A railway horsebox was alongside the Up loading bank, and a road horsebox was nearby; they both had their ramps down and, between them, dancing at the end of a rope held by the lorry driver, was a very frightened horse. John and Maurice were looking on from the safety of their hut; Mr Halford and Basil had put a respectful distance between themselves and the show. The man led the horse up to the railway truck again, Sam waved his arms and made horsy noises but as soon as the animal's hooves touched the ramp it reared and ran out sideways. John and Maurice, behind their window, were delighted.

I went over, brimming with horse-lore. 'Whoa,' I said, professionally, to the horse and 'Give us the rope, mate,' to the bothered, frayed-looking lorry driver.

'You're welcome,' he growled, handing it over.

The horse stood quite still, trembling all over, wondering what this change would mean for it. I spoke quietly to it and stroked its nose before leading it off for a walk around the yard, talking all the while, before circling back and going directly to the box. The horse went straight in.

'Where did you learn that?' asked Mr Halford, gratefully surprised. 'I had three years, part-time, with Dennistoun's race-horses and show-jumpers.'

'So you did – you never know when things will come in useful. How are you getting on with the job? Could you take charge?'

I thought of the ticket business – apart from that I would have taken on immediately and learnt as I went along.

'Well, I'd better have this week and next, Mr Halford.'

'Just as you like,' he said.

'We'll be putting that horsebox on the three o'clock stopper Up,' said Sam. 'You'd better clip the points and couple on. Have you ever coupled passenger stock before?'

'No – hey! You mean the screw link and the vacuum pipes? No, but I've often watched it done, it's something I've always wanted to do.' I felt quite excited at the prospect.

The stopper arrived at 3.10 and two passengers got off. They were obviously railwaymen but of a type I had not seen before, dressed in fine-quality, dark-blue overcoats, shiny black shoes and brown trilby hats. They nodded to Sam as we walked past them to the siding points. 'Afternoon, Sam'. 'Afternoon, Mr Millsom, Mr Lockett.' The points snapped over and I knelt down to screw the clamp on while Sam squatted beside me.

'Who are they then, Sam?'

'Sssh!' he hissed. 'They're watching.'

As the train moved back over the points and hid us from view, Sam said, 'That's Millsom and Lockett – the District Inspector and his assistant. They take you on the rules when you want to be a signalman. They're up now to visit the signal box but they are interested in anything to do with safe working. That's their job.' I thought they looked very pleasant men, one rather short and stocky with a pipe, and the other tall but stout, and could not understand the awe in Sam's voice. However, I was suitably impressed by it and put on my best behaviour to match Sam's. I waved the train back till the buffers clunked. I was in heaven – playing with real trains. Every detail of every passenger shunter's movements I had ever seen at Reading was clear in my mind as I whipped the tail lamp off the rear coach and put it on the ground. Then, ducking under the buffers, I swung the heavy screw coupling up and over the draw-hook of the horsebox and threw the weight round until the coupling was taut so that the buffers would be held firmly together when the train was running. I had a little difficulty with the vacuum pipes; the dextrousness of the Reading shunters had made it seem so easy but my unpractised hands found them stiff and springy. Anyhow, I joined them up and slipped the pin through; then, 'out from under', put the tail lamp on the rear of the horsebox. 'Right Away!'

I was so engrossed that I did not see that the Inspectors and Mr Halford were watching. I scrambled up the loading platform. 'Adrian, this is Mr Millsom, the District Inspector, and this is Mr Lockett, his assistant.' Mr Millsom had very keen, blue eyes and he had an air of calm, gentle authority. I felt immediately that he was what we would have called in the Army a 'good bloke'.

'You managed that job very well, but Mr Halford says you've never done it before.'

'I've spent a lot of time watching, Mr Millsom.'

'Do you think you could "take on" as a porter soon?'

'At the end of two weeks, I think.'

'Very good, you'll do. I hear you want to be a signalman. Have you started reading the regulations?' I said I had not. 'Well, you'd better start; the sooner the better. There's more to a signal box than pulling levers. I'll send you up the rule book and a book of signalling regulations. I'll see you again another day. Good luck. Come on, Jack,' he turned to his portly assistant, 'we'll go up and see Bill.'

I wanted to ask them about Harry's tail lamp riddle, yet it sounded an outlandish question to ask such personages, so I let them go. That evening I saw Albert walk past the office with his dog and bucket on his way to feed his chickens. Although he was as old a hand as Harry and I respected him, I did not feel as if I was talking to a teacher or an officer – which was how everyone felt towards Harry.

'Hey-up, Albert! Hang on, there's something I've got to ask you.' He turned back.

'Hello, Adrian. How's it going? Enjoying yourself?'

'Yes thanks. They say you were over at Patney in the 1920s, Albert.'

'Yes, that's right, 1926 to 1929. I went there from Dauntsey, then I went to Burbage Wharf as porter/signalman until they closed it in the economies in 1931 and came here.'

'So you'd have been on the Berks & Hants line at about the same time as Harry?'

'Well, I think he'd left Woodborough to come here in 1926.'

'Well, it's near enough. He said there was a train he saw every day at Woodborough that had twenty rear lamps. Is that true? I mean, well, I don't suppose he makes up stories but that sounds a bit far-fetched, doesn't it?'

Albert put his bucket down and ran a hand through his hair. 'Well, it does and it doesn't. You've sparked something off up here.' He tapped his head. 'I'm thinking – Ah! Ha! Ha! Old Harry's memory has gone a bit wrong over the years but I know what he means – '

'What is it then?' I asked, almost jumping up and down with the suspense.

'Oh, I'm not telling you. You ask Harry when you see him, "What had seventeen rear lamps and five headlamps?" Tell him I said he was wrong about the twenty lamps and so he'll have to tell you the answer.' He picked up his bucket and went off along the platform, his collie at his heels.

I told Sam and asked, 'Does that make it any clearer to you?'

'No, it doesn't. Rum sort of railway they had then. *Five* headlamps? Even the Royal train only has four.'

On Thursday evening Sam had to take his wife to the doctor so Albert stood in for him for a couple of hours after he had fed his chickens. When he came in I made some tea; his dog lay down in front of the office fire; and with, as I thought, nothing before us but the 8.30 stopper Up, I steered the conversation easily round to the subject of the old days. 'How long have you been on the relief, Albert?'

'Since 1934,' he said proudly. 'I used to go everywhere in the Swindon district from Ludgershall to Cricklade on the old M&SW, from Steventon to Wootton Bassett, up to Highworth and Faringdon and down the Gloucester line as far as Minety.'

'But you haven't got a motorbike even now, how did you get about then?'

'Same as now! Either by train or push bike or a bit of both.'

'Yes, but you couldn't bike to Ludgershall every day from here.'

'You don't believe me? I was supposed to book a lodge if I was sent so far away but I'd rather put that few extra shillings in my wife's housekeeping and cycle each day.'

'Well, you just about earned the extra then.'

'Aha! 'Cos if you were being paid to lodge close by and then you didn't turn up on time they'd naturally want to know why. So you had to be there on time.'

'But whatever time did you get up in the morning to cycle all the way to Ludgershall?'

'Well, to be honest with you, the old Company was too good at its own housekeeping to send men out where they'd have to be paid to lodge. So we didn't often go that far – well, not until the war that is – and then the Government was paying so nobody stopped to count the cost anymore. But before the war I was kept fairly well to my own area, about a ten-mile cycle ride each way, though I did have to go out to Highworth if there was no one closer to do the job.'

'How did you know where to go each week?'

'That was the DI's job – it still is. They get up the orders for all the relief porters and signalmen in the Swindon district, type 'em out on a slip o' paper and you get 'em every Thursday afternoon.'

'What happened during the war? You did more travelling then?'

'Ah well, during the war things went haywire; you got sent off all over the place because of staff shortages. Old Sam's wife, Dot, came over here as a porter, you know.'

'Yes, Sam told me.'

'You see this here?' he asked, tapping his finger on an oval brass badge in his lapel. I looked at it closely.

'Was that a badge to show everyone why you weren't in army uniform? Dad told me that during the first war some women used to go round giving the white feather to any man who wasn't in khaki.'

'Yes, that was often a woman who'd lost a husband or a brother, but we didn't get anything like that in the last lot. No, this badge was our pass to get through police or army road blocks during bombing or anything. Railwaymen were reckoned to be on essential service in them days and had to be allowed to pass.'

'Did you ever have to use it, Albert?'

'Good lord, no! And the essential service was very often no more than ticket collecting. I was five weeks once, booked up at Old Town – blasted well ticket collecting, twelve hours a day ...'

'Old Town? Where's that?'

'You know – Swindon Town station up the top o' Old Town hill, the old M&SW station. I used to cycle all the way there, fifteen or more miles from Challow, and be there by 5.30 in the morning, and tickets – you never saw such piles of tickets; off some o' them trains I'd fill my pockets and then have to take my cap off and fill that.'

'Well, didn't you ask to go somewhere else after a week or two?'

'Huh! You may be sure I did but the old DI just said he was sorry and would I stick it for another week. What could anyone say when there was a war on?'

'So you finished at 5.30 each evening. That'd make it easy to get a train home, I suppose?'

'Oh yes, I could go home on the cushions, and just as well too. I don't think I could have cycled after standing up at the ticket gate all day.'

'What about the station before the war, Albert? Harry has told me a lot about what went on. You had heaps of regular traffic; what about the casual stuff?'

'Did he tell you about our bloody Station Truck?'

'Ha! Ha! Yes, that was pretty crude; did the customers at the groceries know?'

'You know I'm not swearing then, when I say that. Oh, them up at Paddington cleaned it out quite well. I don't remember any complaints but it was a horrible sight when we closed the doors on all them dead horses. Talking of horses, I'll bet he never told you about the race-horses we had here.'

'No, not at all.'

'Aha! Now then, *there* was a casual traffic that was regular. We never knew *who* was coming but we knew some trainer or other *would* come, every day and often for more than one train. Every time there was racing they had to send the horses by rail and we had all the trainers from Childrey, Sparsholt and the two Letcombes.'

'My goodness, that must have been twenty stables – there's six establishments in Childrey even today and one at Sparsholt.'

'Yes, that's old Major Sneyd, been there for years. He had a horse, you know; it could hardly walk on the road but it won nearly all its races – long-distance horse it was. Then there was a Mr Scott from behind the Sparrow pub at Letcombe Regis and Pierrepoint too. Aha! He brought a horse down here one day for Newmarket – the Cesarewitch. There was a hell of a lot of booking to be done on them jobs and costing the price when it went over other companies' lines. Anyhow, this horse was called Myra Grey. I said to the groom, "That couldn't win a camel race." He told me to put my money on it. "No fear!" I said. Huh! It won a 66-1!'

'Well, you know, I was always being given tips by the lads when I was at Dennistoun's but I never had the courage to risk my pocket money.'

'I remember, now you've got me on the subject, there was a Captain Whitelaw at Regis. He used to charter a train for Perth races every year. A saloon for his family, a coach for the staff, six horseboxes and a luggage van – there you are! Old Major West, as he was a Director of the Great Western up at Faringdon, used to have a saloon for Perth races too. It worked up "light" to Faringdon and next day he rode in that right through to Perth.'

I positively *glowed* with excitement. 'My God, Albert – what a railway it was then!'

The door burst open from the yard at that moment and a woman, walking backwards with a pile of cardboard boxes on her hands, came in. She put them on the floor and went out for more, moving so fast that we could only stand back and let her get on with it. She was a little, dark-haired woman, some hair turning grey. 'Coxwell Hatcheries,' said she, slapping a sheet of paper on one of the piles, 'good night.' She went out at a run and slammed the door behind her. She had left fifty cartons of live chicks in the middle of the room. I looked at Albert for an explanation, he shrugged and said, 'That's Meg – she doesn't hang about. Now, this lot has got to be labelled, registered and sorted into "uphills" and "downhills".' He rubbed his horny hands together at the prospect of some work.

Sam came back to let Albert go home just after the 8.30 had left. 'I see now why you had to take your wife to the doctors,' I said when Albert was gone.

'Ah! Don't get the wrong impression. She really did have to go; she had an appointment.'

'Yes, I'm sure she had; you made it and the only free night was tonight.' Sam looked hurt, he was not used to me feeling confident enough to be sarcastic. I could not help laughing. 'Oh, I'm pulling your leg. Anyhow, Albert didn't mind, he was as happy as ...' I stopped. 'Well, he enjoyed it.'

Next week I was on duty with Harry. Calm and order prevailed and I had to wait for a suitable opening to mention the tail lamp business. It was half past eight before we had a break from railway work and could talk about trivialities.

'Did you enjoy your week with Sam?' he asked.

'Yes, I did – there was a lot going on.'

'I'm sure there was,' said Harry drily.

'Er, Albert was here for part of Thursday evening and he says you're wrong about the twenty tail lamps.' Harry's upper lip was down, stiff as a board. 'He said to ask you what had seventeen tail lights and five headlamps.' Harry's lip relaxed. 'Oh dear, I see what he means. I'm afraid I got it wrong; it was a very long time ago.'

'Well, what's it all about then? He said you had to tell me.'

'The train was the 10.30 a.m. Paddington to Penzance – The Cornish Riviera to the public though us chaps called it the "Limited" – don't ask me why, it usually had fifteen coaches. It carried three slips; one was dropped at Westbury for Weymouth, one went off at Taunton and the last was dropped at Exeter. Now, count the lamps. The Westbury had a triple rear light, the other two had doubles – that's seven. Until 1933 passenger trains carried red side lights as well as tail lamps, just as goods trains still do, and each slip coach had side lights – making thirteen lamps so far. The main train had a double red rear light and two side lights, that's seventeen. Now, on top of that you must add a headlamp for each slip and two headlamps for the engine – twenty-two lamps in all.'

'What a performance! All that organisation and complication makes the train seem very grand somehow.'

'Ah. They were grand trains. Fifteen coaches and a big engine all done up with her paint polished and her brasses gleaming. Each slip had its own guard, only the most experienced, because they had to be able to control the coach and bring it to a stand at just the right place after dropping off the train at maybe eighty miles an hour. The "Limited" had five guards.'

'Five? Four surely?'

'No, not in them days.' He stared down at the fire in the stove. 'They had the three slip guards and *two* on the main train, the Junior in the front van and the Head Guard, in charge of the whole train, at the rear. They'd all have their buttonholes, whatever was in season – it might be a daffodil or a rose or carnation – and in their tail coats and wing collars they'd be almost as well dressed as Aldington, the General Manager, the smartest man you ever saw. We used to call them "Aldington's Peacocks".' His voice had died away. 'Those Cornish expresses *were* grand trains.' Suddenly, he straightened. 'But there – it was a long time ago now. We'd better see to today's passengers.' He went out abruptly, into the yard. I didn't follow him but went out onto the platform instead; I did not think he wanted me with him just then.

I do not know where the idea sprang from, but on Tuesday morning it occurred to me that if I went up to Wantage Road on the 8.5 from Challow I could ride back to Challow on the 8.10 from Wantage. I thought I was well enough known to the engine drivers to be able to ask for the ride; it seemed like an interesting distraction and one I should not be able to enjoy once I was the porter on duty at the station.

Each morning that week I rode on the footplate of the 'Castle' on the 8.5 from Challow and made the discovery that the enginemen had a game of their own. This was to accelerate their eight-coach train with such precision that 60 mph was reached exactly as Circourt IBS home signal, one and a half miles from start, was passed. Brutal acceleration would have taken us up to 60 in less than the distance with this moderate load but, played properly, it was a skilful game – though by its nature, a short one.

The throttle, or, to give it its railway-correct name, the regulator, was shut as we flashed past the signal and we would freewheel the one and three quarter miles to Wantage Road where the Down train was on the point of leaving. I would climb down off the 'Castle', dash across the tracks and climb onto the footplate of a '61' or '63' class engine – I never knew what type to expect. Indeed, on Tuesday morning it occurred to me, only as I was crossing the lines, that the driver of the engine might not want me on his engine but luckily he was a man I knew from the Fly – he was rather surprised when I suddenly appeared in the cab but did not mind.

On arrival at Challow I could be ushering the girls onto the train and slamming doors before Mr Halford had crossed the bridge, or Harry had finished with the parcels lorry.

Two large, brown-paper parcels were lying on the office table, addressed to me, when I arrived for work on Friday. 'Your uniform has come,' said Harry. 'We'll have to see how you look in it later on, after the 10.30 Up.'

At the time he suggested we had a spare half-hour, the Fly had gone away and there was nothing to be loaded at the goods shed. 'Come on then, let's see your new uniform.'

'Well, I don't know, Harry, surely it's the same as yours. I'll take it home and try it.'

Mr Halford and Basil appeared in the door. 'Yes, but you'll be on your own next week. Harry won't be here to see how you look.'

'Am I taking on next week then, Mr Halford?'

'That's what you told Mr Millsom and me the other day; you'll be all right, I think.' I thought of those tickets, shoved the thought aside in the excitement of doing all the practical, outdoor work myself, in my smart new uniform. 'Right then,' I said, 'let's see what we've got.' I opened a parcel. It contained my overcoat. 'Oh! It's very heavy.'

'They always are; made of very good stuff,' said Mr Halford. 'Try it on.' The door opened at that moment and Sam Loder came in. The office was full of men. They stood around me in a half-circle – looking expectant.

'What do you think this is? The *Folies Bergère*? I'm not stripping, only trying an overcoat.'

I put it on. 'Hooray!' They all yelled except Harry, and even he smiled. It was like a bell-tent – right down to the floor. 'Try the other things,' urged Sam. I remembered then that he and Halford had taken the measurements and there had been a funny look on Loder's face. 'You rotten sods!' I yelled and opened the other package.

The jacket was too narrow across the shoulders by a mile and the sleeves were like hosepipes, the trousers were, as Harry put it, 'either long shorts or short longs' and made his rare 'whoofing' sort of laugh from under his stiff upper lip – the waistcoat would have been too small for a leprechaun. I held each piece up so they could have a good laugh. The remarkable thing was the extreme impossibility of the fit; whoever had read Sam's original measurements had realised that someone was being 'sent up' and entered into the spirit of the thing. The three-piece suit must have been held up and caused similar mirth in some clothing factory in London the week before.

It was a good joke but left me feeling very disappointed because I had been looking forward to coming to work all bulled up. I had even bought a piece of silver chain for the waistcoast – now I should have to wait another three weeks before I got a suit.

'Never mind, Adrian,' said Mr Halford, still smiling. 'Take another form home and get your mother to run over you with a tape measure – you can borrow the spare cap when you are in charge on late turn next week.'

Before I finished work that Friday, the last time Harry and I would ever work together, he said to me, 'I should keep that overcoat, when you re-order, it'll come in very handy when you go riding on engines.' He looked very stern from under his peaked cap. 'Take care of yourself – and don't forget the old 10.30 "Limited".'

Chapter Ten

Pleasures of a Day

Constant journeying over the two and a half miles of lane between the village and the station taught me every bump and bend in the road. I could have driven there with my eyes shut, not that I ever tried, but in the thick fogs of November – the next thing to driving 'blind' – it was encouraging to be able to use each bump or sideways roll as a definitive marker; over the canal bridge, count ten, hit the filled-in trench, bear left, feel the sudden, steep camber of the road and brake for the bend. I deliberately developed this skill because it was similar to the technique used by engine drivers to keep their bearings in dense fog.

The journey was always a pleasure, to see the familiar road in every type of weather and through the changing seasons; the racehorse stables and the old, grey tower of the parish church; the roadside elms and the elmy hedgerows frothing with cow-parsley; Tommy Carter's farm, approaching which at a quarter to seven in the morning I would meet his cows ambling messily to milking herded by his slim, blonde daughter with the brilliant smile; past Petwick Stud and on, through the last twisting half mile to the main road and the station. All the scenes from childhood left behind on the daily drive to work.

It was also a pleasure to drive my Morris, even if, on the coldest winter nights I had to travel with a blanket round my legs and a hot-water bottle in my lap. Those small, gentle, pre-war cars were friendly machines, lacking in power so that you actually had to think ahead when you drove them, to work up speed for the hills, lacking that 'float along' comfort which insulates the modern driver from the road – often with fatal results.

But the old car had her peculiar temptations – she had a device on the dashboard for screwing open the throttle and a 'sunshine' sliding roof; it was possible to set the throttle, climb onto the roof and steer with my feet. In that quiet lane I used to drive most of the way home in this manner. It seemed a good idea at the time and was very exciting but on the last occasion I did this a car approached from the opposite direction and its driver, seeing an apparently driverless car approaching with its passenger sitting on the roof, took swift but ill-judged evasive action and crashed into the hedge.

Mr Halford let me get on with the portering work at the station and rarely interfered; not even when Basil complained loudly that I had, yet again, made a nonsense in his beautifully kept ledgers. I never mastered the accounts side of the business but I thoroughly enjoyed the practical, outdoor railway work and many impressions of it remain with me today.

On dark winter mornings the first passengers would arrive, with gruff early-morning greetings, while I was winching the Tilley lamps into place above the platform gate and under the awning. Old Joe, hobbling beside his bicycle, his long, craggy face and hooked nose looking grimmer than ever as he passed from shadow to the harsh light of the Tilley and into shadow again, the building labourers, pale and stubbly black around their chins, waiting for their tickets.

At 7.20, while I was attending to their fares, the 3-1 code rang out. 'That's your train, gentlemen, just off Uffington.' They would grunt 'Thanks' and go back to the platform.

Four minutes later the locomotive's single headlamp appeared out of the darkness; the rolling exhaust smoke coloured by the engine's white-hot fire. In another minute the locomotive and its three carriages came spanking into the station, I saw a flash of firelight as the engine slid darkly past, I heard a squeal of iron brake-blocks on steel wheels – stop. After the commotion of arrival the silence seemed profound, steam wreathed up from beneath the carriages, past yellow-lit, fogged windows. Then I heard the hiss of the locomotive's safety-valves at full pressure and the gurgling whistle of the boiler water-injectors at work.

The guard and I helped Joe up into the van with his bike, the labourers, bulky in shiny-backed woollen overcoats, climbed into the train and the guard handed me some railway letters. 'Where's old Harry today then?'

'I've taken on now. I'm on my own.'

'Oh ah! How d'you get on with him then?'

'One of the best, I think.'

'One of the real old school is Harry. Are we right?' I went to the carriage doors and checked them, turned and raised my hand to the guard.

Standing on the platform, the door of his van open, the guard turned his hand-lamp to green and blew his whistle. I heard the fireman's 'Right Away, mate!' to his driver, the prompt 'toot' on the engine's whistle, the first 'whoofs' of the exhaust. With such a light load, acceleration was rapid. The guard jumped aboard – almost too late, it seemed – his door swinging shut with the rapid forward movement of the train. He gave me a wave and disappeared inside.

The engine on that train would be an ex-works machine, anything from a 'King' to a 'Manor'. I never grew tired of watching the receding train, especially on dark, cold mornings, listening to the chattering, changing rhythm of the exhaust coming back through the chilly air. The red tail lamp flickered as the coach jarred over each rail joint and the cold, green signal lamps changed to baleful red as the train passed them and the signalman restored the arm to 'Danger'.

The scene was rooted in the eighteenth-century days of stagecoach travel. The passengers in their narrow compartments, each one with three small windows in the side, the Guard, in charge of the train – his narrow door lettered in black and gold on a maroon ground – the Driver, with his undoubtedly horse-like engine, brassy as a well-polished harness. The clatter and commotion of the train's arrival and departure had the dash, the *élan* of a stagecoach rattling over the cobbles into an old inn yard; the High Speed Train is very much faster (though it will not take you to Challow) but it is not dashing.

Even the phrases we used came from coaching days. An engine working hard uphill was said to be 'in the collar', the collar being a piece of harness around the horse's neck to which the shafts of the cart were attached and against which the animal pulled. The working timetable directed 'Engine to take water', as if it went to a trough to drink; indeed, there were places where locomotive water *was* taken from troughs while the train was running. Engines and trains, even the Royal train, were 'stabled' on a siding. The Fly, I discovered at last, took its name from a one-horse, light cart used for short journeys with many stops.

The parcels lorry was a pre-war Thorneycroft driven by a decrepit man known jovially as 'Lightning'. He took snuff in larger quantities than was good for him and his nose often showed signs of recent bleeding while his waistcoat was permanently stained black and tan from years of fallout. He was not jovial and his early morning gloom always deepened at the sight of a nineteen-year-old porter. He had his job worked out to a fine art and my inexperience must have been very trying for him. As we loaded his lorry, he kept up a barrage of protest. 'No, not that one, that goes on last. No, no, not there, that's me Charneys and you're mixing 'em wi' the Gooseys. Wait, wait, you're mucking up the whole system. What's yer rush?'

I wanted to be on the platform in time to say a few words to the girls and usher them onto the train. I would then slam their carriage doors professionally, call 'Right Away' in my best, parade-ground voice and send the train off with a commendable show of masterful efficiency.

When I got back to the office, Lightning would have taken the delivery sheet I had made out and departed, leaving behind a snuffy thumb-print on the desk where the sheet had laid. It was breakfast-time now, so, dusting all surfaces first, I laid out my food and switched on the kettle.

I tried to follow Harry's example and be at the goods shed to meet the Fly on its way back from Uffington. If the signalman forgot to ring it in, it would signal its own arrival by a sudden loud roar as it rolled over some rail lengths alongside the goods shed wall. A platelayer told me that the noise was due to the curiously worn surface of the rails which had been used inside the sulphurous Severn Tunnel for many years; there was nothing I could see but they made a terrific din with the goods shed as an enormous sounding box and echo chamber.

The train stopped with a lot of clashing ringing from its cymbal-like buffers, striking and rebounding, coupling chains snatching and tugging horribly. The points into the yard were reversed, buffers rang again, this time in an orderly progression, as with hoarse, hollow chuffs the '37' class tank engine closed up its train, the front moving while the back stood still till the guard's van moved and the train set back into the siding. The points were reversed again and the shunting could begin.

Shunting was always a pleasant half-hour for me. I enjoyed working closely with a steam engine and the feeling of teamwork as the driver, fireman, guard and myself worked by handsignals. As I write I can hear the cracking, grinding noise peculiar to old sidings when locomotives move slowly over them. The train was manned by Didcot men with a Didcot-based engine; there were, perhaps, five men in the 'link' that worked the job – they also worked the Didcot–Swindon stopping passenger trains – so that in ten weeks I had worked with them all and my place on their footplate was assured.

When I was booked as late turn porter I could join the Fly at 7 a.m. and have three hours in the company of the unfailingly cheerful enginemen, travelling down to Uffington and back, often as 'fireman' and sometimes being allowed to drive.

A driver once handed over his '22' class engine to me in Challow yard saying, 'Look out now, you've only got the steam-brake on the engine, the tender's unbraked.' All went well until we had to go into Goosey Dock to pick up a wagon. I braked a second too late. The engine stopped nicely but the 35 tons of unbraked tender gave a mighty shove which drove the engine into the wagon which was hard against the buffers and threw the three of us against the firebox and its hot, copper pipes. The driver was upset and said so. The skill of the job was to make allowances for everything.

Part of a goods guard's skill was to arrange the work so as to carry it out in as few movements as possible: the staff magazine used to carry shunting puzzles with a time limit on solving them and men were proud of their reputation for clever shunting and dextrous use of the pole. I once heard a man mentioned who was so proud of his job as a shunter that he used to go to chapel each Sunday with his pole over his shoulder so that everyone should know what his job was.

When wagons were standing in odd little sidings all round the yard, it was often necessary to have trucks before and behind the engine and fly-shunting came into use. Fly-shunted wagons were drawn along not pushed. The man uncoupling put his pole into position before the train started and raised his free arm for the driver to start. He ran alongside until he judged the moment right to uncouple, signalled to the driver to ease-up, the coupling slackened as steam was shut off, the shunter slipped the link off the hook and waved the driver away.

The engine accelerated vigorously so that it cleared the points well before the wagons following loose behind. This gave space in which the man at the points could operate the lever and divert the trundling raft. Siding points were always uneven so speed was essential if the trucks were to have sufficient momentum to overcome the lumps, bumps and flange-squealing friction and pass clear into the siding. If they stopped across the points they blocked the other line and possibly penned the engine into a dead-end.

If that happened we used the pinch-bar to lever the trucks clear or we might ask the coal merchant to pull them with his lorry – this was illegal but it never stopped us from doing it. If this problem arose, it did so right outside the stable which once housed Harry's shunting horse, Duchess, and I often looked up at it while we puffed away with the pinch-bar and wished she was still in there.

During any weekday in 1960, eight titled trains passed Challow in each direction. Two were the blue and white Pullman diesels – like bullet-nosed rail-cars. They had started their public service on the same day that I started learning the portering job at Challow. The other six were locomotive-hauled with cream and brown coaches – and five of them were steam-hauled. After nationalisation in 1948 the Great Western coach livery of chocolate and cream gave way to Socialist red and yellow – 'rhubarb and custard' – but in 1954, when revolutionary ardour had cooled and common sense began to reassert itself, the old colours were reintroduced, starting with the coaches for the named expresses.

The man behind this was Reginald Hanks, the last Great Western railwayman to be in charge at Paddington. He had served an engineering apprenticeship at the Great Western factory at Swindon before the First World War, had fought in that war and afterwards went to work for William Morris, later Lord Nuffield, becoming Works Manager at Cowley before taking the post of Chairman of the Board of Western Region at Paddington.

He was unique as a Chairman of the railway in that he regularly fired the engine that took his train from Oxford to Paddington – indeed, it was said that he had his overalls hanging behind the Boardroom door and would terminate a meeting with 'You must excuse me gentlemen – I'm firing the Cornish Riviera this morning.' Sir Daniel Gooch had often driven engines as Locomotive Superintendent in the 1840s and '50s but it is very doubtful if he shovelled coal when he became the Chairman of the Board.

The named expresses were:

The Bristolian
The South Wales Pullman
The Bristol Pullman
The Pembroke Coast Express
The Merchant Venturer
The Capitals United
The Cheltenham Spa Express
The Red Dragon

Reggie Hanks's expresses were a sight for sore eyes. The green, brass and copper polished locomotive carried before its chimney a decorative headboard bearing the train's title and hauled a row of cream and brown coaches. The sturdy old atmosphere was completed by the yards-long destination boards which the coaches carried above the line of their windows, a most useful practice to the public and one with its origins in the days of stagecoach travel. I enjoyed reading the fine-sounding names, English, Cornish and Welsh, romantic with distance, ringing with poetry – 'THE PEMBROKE COAST EXPRESS. PADDINGTON TENBY & PEMBROKE DOCK' sounded like a proud boast of the train's daily achievement while it had a noble alliterative effect when I read it to the rhythm of the wheels' rapid tattoo as they drummed through the station.

The first big diesel locomotives on Western Region – the 'Warship' class – appeared in 1958. They were not reliable and earned the name 'Growlers' very quickly but they were the latest thing, and in the summer of 1959 the Bristolian was scheduled for 'Warship' haulage and had five minutes cut from its very fast schedule. 'Warship' failures ensured that the train occasionally had steam power, probably the most remarkable incident being when the Down Bristolian failed at Reading sometime in 1960.

A '28' class goods engine was the only spare available and was coupled to the front of the dead diesel with the intention that it should haul the train to Swindon where a 'Castle' would take over. The '28' class design dated from 1903 and had 4-foot 7 ½-inch-diameter driving wheels for hauling very heavy goods trains; steam engines for high-speed running had wheels 6 feet 6 inches or more in diameter. The '28' did exceptionally well, running at 60 mph with the 370-ton train but soon after passing Didcot the 'Warship' came to life and began to push the goods engine into Bristolian-style speed.

I saw the train at Challow. The old '28' had the Bristolian headboard up and was probably travelling at 80 mph. It looked absolutely terrifying as its long side-rods were driven round by the tiny, more or less invisible driving wheels but the '28''s driver threw a note out as he passed Challow box – 'No relief at Swindon.'

The entire station staff turned out to see the engine pushed over the maze of Swindon's point work, the signalmen at Dauntsey and Box said that the train was running at normal speed at the foot of both inclines yet it arrived safely at Bristol, the '28' clanking loudly into the station, her headboard still proudly in position.

At the west end of the platform an ambulance party of fitters, foremen and Locomotive Superintendent were waiting and a pair of steam cranes were standing by in the shed in case the '28' had to be lifted off the track! But they were not needed and the old engine ran back to Swindon factory for examination under her own power. I never heard if any defects were found.

The lunch hour at Challow became increasingly hazardous as Basil and Maurice became more ambitious in their jokes until they overstepped the mark. There was a splendid, official brass pass-key to the public lavatory on the platform which saved us paying pennies to the railway. One lunchtime I took it along to the door but found the closet occupied and returned. As I opened the door from the platform I saw the far door closing – oh, so quietly! – and caught a glimpse of a fire bucket through the diminishing gap. Basil and Maurice had noticed the missing pass-key and thought they had young Ady sitting pretty.

A moment later there came a great splash as the contents of the bucket were hurled through the lavatory ventilator, followed by the outraged shout of the victim. From the jokers' point of view, a very satisfactory reaction. The sound of tiptoeing footsteps came close, the door opened and in tumbled Basil and Maurice, bursting with suppressed laughter – until they saw me sitting by the fire. The change that came over their faces was a joy to watch.

Squelching noises now came along the platform, we ducked down behind the table to see who had been caught and saw one of the coal merchant's men go by

– a big man to be throwing water over but he never complained. Our clever pair gave that game up and contented themselves with putting glue on door handles, tying dustbins to cars' rear bumpers and nailing caps to table tops.

One night I was on duty when the 5.5 Paddington came down with fifteen coaches and would not fit our platform; either the front or rear three coaches would stop over open track. There was also the risk that it would come to a stand with the tail standing out over the power points from the Down main to platform, so the signalmen arranged to run it down the relief line from Wantage Road and for me to stand at the east end of the platform and yell instructions to passengers *not* to get off at the rear but to walk four coaches forward.

No one appeared to get off except at the platform and we complimented ourselves on the efficiency of our arrangements; the train left and I went back to the office. Five minutes later a dishevelled – and rather deaf – old gentleman tottered into the room. 'Just stepped off a train, sir?' The unkind question was smothered just before it broke surface as he said, 'The last time I travelled by train, young man, it stopped at the platform.' How anyone could step off the brink into total darkness was more than I could understand. 'Surely one is obliged to look where one is going, sir?' Olde worlde haughtiness showed beneath his layer of dust and creosote. 'I shall sue you for this,' he snapped. But luckily he did not. I am sure he would have lost.

Once the Down fast had gone, there was nothing much to do except read a book and wait for telephone calls from prospective customers – and on Thursday, see to thousands of live chicks. One evening the telephone rang.

'Hello, Cha ...'

A loud voice cut in with 'Where's my damned caviar?' The accents were thick from too much brandy consumed in the past hour and the past forty years and were instantly recognisable as belonging to a military gentleman who lived out in the Vale.

Only just resisting the temptation to share his mood and tear a strip off a military gentleman – after all, I *was* fresh from the Army – I said, 'Can I have your name please, sir?' He gave it and repeated his inelegant request for the elegant food. We worked out together that it was being delivered by British Road Services whereupon he slammed the telephone down without another word. Next Christmas, among the seasonal gifts of rabbits and £1 notes from the local gentry was a brace of pheasants addressed to 'The Porters at Challow Station'. They had come with the compliments of my caviar cavalier – not that I ate either of them, I was no longer at the station when they arrived!

The solitude of the evening porter's position made a blank sheet for indelible impressions. I loved the rainy, windswept winter evenings when the wet platforms gleamed under the harsh light of the Tilleys, their garishness accentuating the surrounding inky blackness. And out of the dark would thunder the 'Kings' and 'Castles', showering fire, their brasswork catching momentarily the station lights, their long trains of yellow-lit coaches blurring past to the sound of the rail joints' rhythm – till, suddenly, there was only steam and smoke swirling and rolling under the platform canopy and the sound of the wind in the telephone wires.

The last train of the day, the 9.30 Down, had only one regular customer, a man called Jetsam, who had a brother, so I was told, called Flotsam, whom I never met. Jetsam worked at a nearby scrapyard, and as I was often there, looking for bits for my Morris, we had become good friends. He came to the station each evening, bought a ticket to Shrivenham for himself and his bike and helped me finish the last of the tea. I never saw him get off a morning train so I presumed he cycled fifteen miles to work each day.

Most Saturday nights a man and woman came up from Swindon on the 4.30 stopper. They would walk away from the station, arm in arm, as civil as you please but when they came back to catch the 9.30 they would be swearing and screaming at each other and calling on the porter to hear the argument and judge between them. The routine never varied.

Getting them into the train was very difficult because the coaches were the compartment, non-corridor type and they would refuse to sit together but when I placed them in the separate compartments of their choice, one would leap out and try to get in with the other. The guard would lend a hand, and sometimes a boot because he was not shy of them as I was; the train would go on its way leaving me to gather up his lamps, two at a time, lock the station and go home to bed.

Nine months passed at Challow, a happy time. The work was enjoyable; I had good company around me and a constant procession of handsome locomotives and trains to watch; the signal box was available to me at any time of the day. My life at work was simply an extension of my play of the last fifteen years – and I was being paid for it! It is a remarkable fact that the engines in service in 1960, whilst not the actual ones that were in service before 1914, were very similar and would have been perfectly familiar to my grandfather; the spirit that moved the railwaymen I knew was just as old-fashioned and conservative. Life was secure, the scene was set as firmly as the elm trees in the hedgerows and would go on forever and ever, Amen.

Chapter Eleven

Elwyn's Way

But I wanted to be a signalman. I studied the lists of vacancies that appeared once a fortnight and applied when a job at Uffington box was advertised. As there was less overtime at Uffington than anywhere else on the line and as it was rated at Class 3 for pay, like most other boxes in the area, no one else applied and I got the job. This caused a few eyebrows to be raised, and Harry Strong told me that I was going into a signal box after only nine months on the railway whereas, before the war, men waited nine years for a tiny, Class 6 box. Mr Millsom was so alarmed by this precipitate promotion that he ruled out my working at Uffington until I had spent some time at Lockinge. 'There's a lot of points and signals at Uffington, Adrian,' he told me seriously, 'you'd be better off going to Lockinge for a year, just to get the hang of things.'

Lockinge, absolutely remote on a high embankment, between Wantage Road and Steventon, the wide Vale and the sky, reached through farmyards and field paths, could have been a good place to work but for the fact that it had only four levers and nothing to do with them all day but pull them over and throw them back for each train. I prepared for a very boring year, but the morning I was to start to learn the box, it was shut and so I went to Uffington after all.

There were two ways to reach Uffington box from Childrey – via Challow station and Baulking through flat country or via Kingstone Lisle, a hilly road for most of the way. By the former route I could almost guarantee the sight of a steam engine; nearly every time I drew up at the junction of the Childrey lane and the main road, there would be a plume of steam rising from the engine of a goods train waiting on the Down relief line for a 'path' to Swindon. On this road I was able to wave to Bill Mattingley as he passed from Uffington village to Challow station; signalmen spent eight hours a day working with each other over their instruments but rarely met and so they valued these brief encounters.

This was the only route on winter Monday mornings, I was told, when snow had fallen or there had been an intense frost during the night. The road passed close to Uffington's Down distant signal, which was a semaphore arm worked by a wire; when the signal box was switched out over the weekend and the arm lowered to show 'All Clear' it often froze in that position. So the wise signalman would get out of his car and walk across the field to jump on the wire and move the signal arm; when he entered the signal box and threw the distant signal's lever over, the arm and wire, being free of ice, would return to the 'Caution' position.

The Kingstone Lisle route took me along the Roman Portway with fine views of the Berkshire Downs to the south and the Vale to the north and through the magnificent avenue of beech on Captain Lonsdale's land. The majority of signal boxes are, or were, deep in the countryside and part of the pleasure of working them was derived from the view you had of the meadows, the birds and animals, the sunrises and sunsets, the weather and the drive to and from home.

Uffington station was the least attractive place at which I have worked. It was built in a style which I call post-Brunellian-gloomy-gothic down in a cutting and had a wide awning that kept all but the most persistent sunbeams out of its dark brown interior. It was situated at the western end of Baulking cutting and was overshadowed by tall trees and the large, red-brick Junction Hotel. I felt a curiously dull atmosphere about the place, even on sunny days. There was a stillness which probably had something to do with the monstrous elms and the grim, green fir trees across the road, which overpowered or stifled all other feelings, but I was not surprised to learn that there had been at least one suicide there, one unexplained death and several obviously accidental ones.

The station had known better times, when the Faringdon branch had a real purpose and people used trains from necessity. Had events worked out as planned, there would have been a much larger station here for Dr Beeching to close: had the Faringdon line continued through Fairford to Cheltenham as intended in 1860 and if the Great Western had completed the Didcot–Wootton Bassett quadrupling scheme of 1900. Some half-finished earthworks for this can still be seen on the up side of the line after the 69 mile post and the existing steel bridge which carried the lane over the site of the station has a span of 109 feet – enough to span four tracks and a couple of sidings as well.

The signal box was built on the Up platform just east of the station office, almost opposite the 66 ½ mile post and was a handsome, timber building dating from 1897. A short flight of steps led down to the door of the interlocking room and another short flight led up from the platform to the door of the operating room. I walked up these steps on a fine, summer morning and was greeted at the door by the man who was going to teach me the job, Elwyn Richards.

He was stocky, about 5 feet 6 inches tall, forty-seven years old, his dark hair cut short at the back and sides, swept severely away from his forehead and parted with perfect accuracy to one side. He was wearing railway-issue, blue serge trousers and waistcoat, polished black shoes, and a collarless, black-striped flannel shirt, the sleeves of which were rolled up to show a pair of very useful-looking forearms. He thrust out his right hand, his smile and his glasses flashed together and in a soft, Welsh voice he said, 'You're A-dren. I'm pleased to meet you, come in.'

I stepped inside. 'Pleased to meet you – at last. I've heard your name often enough when I've been in Challow box.' The room was rather dark. The cutting bank rose opposite the front windows, which were, in any case, partly blocked by the row of levers; the 'lever frame' and the west window were partially blocked

Uffington station as it looked at any time between 1952 and 1964. The station was opened in 1864 for the Faringdon branch, which can be seen curving away to the north. The signal box was rebuilt on the platform in 1896. With the withdrawal of passenger trains on the branch in December 1951, the station name board was changed to plain 'Uffington' rather than 'Uffington Junction for Faringdon'and several signals, on the branch line side, were removed. But still – working at Uffington was pleasantly going back in time. (R. M. Casserley)

Uffington looking east from the Down main line. (R. M. Casserley)

The 1896-vintage, forty-seven-lever frame at Uffington. The levers were mutually interlocked by a remarkably cumbersome mechanism designed in 1890 by a GWR engineer. This design was a modification of an 1870 design. The locks were moved on and off the levers by giving each one a pair of rollers through which passed a flat, metal bar with a twist at each end. When the lever was pulled over or pushed back, the rollers passed over the twisted bar, causing it to rotate and thus movement was given to the locking bars. I used to take up one of the metal covers at the foot of a lever so as to watch the action of the rollers and bar as I pulled the lever. Everything about the mechanical railway was fascinating. (Author)

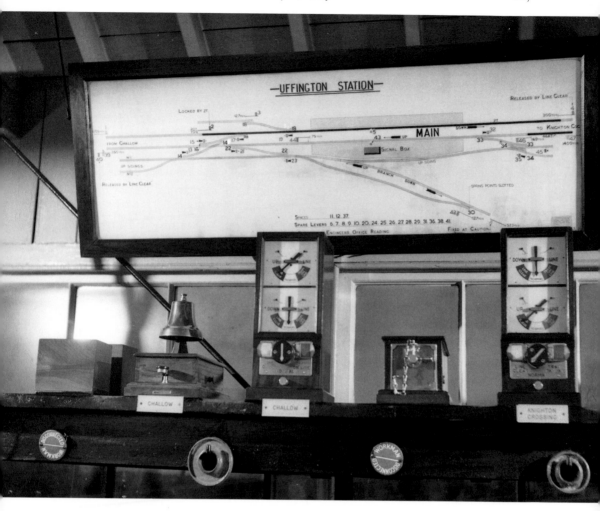

The track diagram, hand-drawn and coloured in, hanging over the 1947-style GWR block signalling instruments. The right-hand instrument works with Knighton Crossing signal box and shows, in the lower section, that I have given 'Line Clear' on the Up line to Knighton so that he can lower his signals for a train to approach Uffington. The left-hand instrument shows that I have asked Challow if the line is clear at his box for the train to approach him, he has sent me 'Line Clear' and consequently I have cleared my signals. Besides the block instruments are the signalling bells. Between the instruments is the 'block switch' by means of which I can 'switch out of circuit', clear my Up and Down line signals and make the 'block section' Challow–Knighton Crossing. 1961. (Author)

by the station's awning, which came within ten feet of the glass. The back wall of the box faced north and had only one square window at each end, so most of the levers, the instruments on the shelf above them and the diagram of the tracks controlled from the signal box were in shadow. Elwyn must have read my face, for he drew down the corners of his mouth deprecatingly. 'Dark 'ole this. Closed in like. The station's u-*ri*-nals are right outside the window; in summer now, we 'ave to keep on at George to keep them swilled out properly or they'd smell.'

He drew a tin from his waistcoat pocket, using his thumb and forefinger in a characteristic movement and offered it to me – it was an enamelled snuff box. 'Go on, 'ave some. It's carnation scented, clear your head a treat.'

'It'd probably blow my head off altogether, thanks Elwyn.'

He drew down his mouth in a quick grimace and snuffed each nostril, giving an exaggerated gasp of satisfaction for my edification. 'You can have the middle locker for your traps,' he said, stepping across to a row of three cupboards that were placed against the back wall between the window and the stove. They were painted brown with cream panels under a single, black top. He opened the central door. 'Oh drat!' An avalanche of half-pint Guinness bottles crashed down around his feet and went flooding, clanking away across the lino floor; there must have been two dozen at least.

'Who drank that lot?' I asked as we scrambled across the floor, gathering them up.

'Me, I forgot about 'em. I like to 'ave a half with my sandwiches in the evenings. Missus across the way in the pub leaves a half on top of the bank; it's handy to her kitchen window, and that saves me having to find time to go all round to the bar. I'd better take 'em back.'

I put my teapot, mug and other bits into the empty cupboard. Elwyn's tea-making equipment was on top of the cupboard, under the telephones that were screwed to the wall. There was one connected to the station at Faringdon, another for the 'omnibus' line which connected all the signal boxes from Foxhall Junction (Didcot) to Highworth Junction (Swindon) and the mahogany-boxed 'Control' phone.

'I'll make us some tea,' said Elwyn. 'Do you take sugar?'

'Yes please, but let's use my stuff.'

'Mine this time, yours the next, that's fair. I expect you know what everything is but look around and ask if you want to know anything –' A deep-sounding bell rang. 'That'll be the "Swansea" I expect – answer it.'

I looked at the two block bells. The Challow bell was a 'church dome', a traditional bell shape which was high-pitched, so the Knighton bell must have rung, this being a 'flat dome' bell giving the deep note. I tapped the Knighton tapper once and back came four bells for an express train. I returned the code and turned the handle of the block indicator to 'Line Clear'.

'Shall I ask on to Challow, Elwyn?'

'Not yet. Wait till you get the "Approach" from Knighton; that's sent when the fast's off Ashbury.'

I began to take in more of the box. The floor measured about 35 feet by 12, giving plenty of room around the forty-seven levers, many of which were painted white – out of use. 'What did all these do, Elwyn?'

'They were finished with when the branch was closed to passengers and the signals were taken away and the points took off the frame and made into hand-operated levers on the ground. Look here.' He went to one of the back windows and slid it open. We looked out, along the branch platform and down the branch line, which curved sharply northwards away from the station towards Faringdon. 'There was a starting signal over there between the run-round loop and the bank, and out on the bend there was an advanced starting signal with one of the old shunt-ahead arms with a big S on the arm. That way,' he pointed into the cutting towards Challow, 'there was a bracket signal to go out on the main line or up into the sidings, and in the run-round loop we had a throw-off point at each end and there was a lot more besides.'

The deep-sounding bell rang 1-2-1 just then. 'There's the "Approach" from Knighton get the road and pull off.' I tapped once on the Challow tapper, back came one ding on the Challow bell, I tapped out four beats, back came the code and the block indicator for Challow turned to 'Line Clear'. I could now lower the Up line signals. I looked at the brass plate on the distant signal lever. This gave the levers that had to be pulled before the distant signal could be operated – 40, 44 and 46, then the Up distant, 47. I heaved them over rather awkwardly because I had to learn the pulling characteristics of each one.

Levers were more or less difficult to pull depending on what they operated, points, bolts or signal arms and upon the distance of those items from the box. Manually operated points could not be more than 350 yards away but signals might be 1,300 yards from the box; the wire passing round several pulleys as it crossed tracks and carried up signal posts, which made for friction and consequently a heavy pull. Replacing a point lever was as light, or heavy, as pulling it but signal levers were always easy to replace owing to the tension of the wire; often they would fly back across the frame when the holding latch was released with a blow from the heel of the hand.

It was not a matter of brute strength. I have watched with amusement a burly policeman struggling with a signal lever, managing to get it half way over before it overpowered him and fell back into the row, dragging him with it.

In replacing a lever, a strong spring beneath the floor was compressed, which then helped to throw the lever over when it was next pulled. The feet had to be correctly placed, the right on the floor slightly to one side, the left on the cast-iron treads, the lever and the man's spine directly in line. If the pull was a heavy one, the signalman swung backwards from the hips, making use of all available acceleration provided by the spring and any slack in the wire to gather momentum to overcome the increasing friction of the wire. He then finished the pull momentarily off balance – it was only for a fraction of a second but it could be dangerous.

A light pull would entail no more than releasing the lever's latch, allowing the spring to throw the lever half way over the frame from where a gentle pressure from the signalman would finish the movement. In pulling four levers, both types would be found with variations between.

Levers were always pulled with a duster. This prevented sweat from hands rusting the carefully polished steel handles and also made pulling more comfortable and easier because the handle had to move in the hands, which it could not do when gripped tightly in bare fists. Not any rag did for this job but a proper duster – a square of soft, cotton cloth woven with red, light and dark blue lines. The design had not changed in living memory – only the initials, and even in 1960 I was the proud owner of a duster with the magic cipher GWR woven into it.

The duster was the signalman's unofficial badge of office and if more than one signalman was in a signal box – say on an engineering Sunday when extra men were drafted in to help – the 'on-duty officer' could be instantly recognised by the duster hanging from his trouser pocket or draped over one shoulder. In the very rare event of a signalman having to be removed from a signal box instantly, perhaps after a crash when he might be in a state of shock and not fit to continue work, his Inspector would say, 'You'd better give me the duster, Fred.'

Two beats from the Knighton bell signified that the 'Swansea' was passing Knighton and was 'on line' to us at Uffington. I acknowledged the code and turned the block indicator to 'Train on Line'. 'Here,' said Elwyn, 'I've got the tea ready and I've been doing the book but now you're here I may as well let you get on with it. I'll sit down with my cup. You better book that "on line" you've just had.'

The railway line was divided into sections and no train was permitted to enter a section without the permission of the controlling signalman. All equipment concerned directly with signalling trains through the sections had the prefix 'block'; thus we had 'block sections' and 'block register', officially the 'train register' or, to the signalman, 'the book'. It was a very important part of the proceedings and in it the time of every bell code received or sent, every unusual occurrence, equipment failure or special message was recorded. Most, if not all, signalmen took pains to keep the record accurately, minute by minute as the codes rang out and some men, especially those who had started as booking boys in large signal boxes took pride in writing very neatly. Properly kept, the register was an aid to memory and vital evidence in the case of an accident.

The Up train came tearing past; it felt strange to have it running so close to the box after the spacious layout at Challow. I put two levers back, sent the two beats to Challow, spotted the tail lamp, sent the 'Train out of Section' 2-1 to Knighton and replaced the last levers. As I wrote the times in the book, Elwyn said, 'You'll 'ave difficulty getting the tail lamps here what with one thing an' another so always try to pick 'em out right outside the box, don't wait till they've gone past. The Up trains get mixed up with the water column and the station nameboard and the down ones get smothered in smoke between the station buildings. Actually, its OK now but there's plenty of times when it isn't, so it's best to get into the right habit now.'

'Righto then, Elwyn. I like your track circuit repeaters in their nice, brass cases. I've never seen instruments like that before.'

'They must be quite old – course, you had "all balls" at Challow.'

'Yes, but at Wantage Road they had red lights in the diagram to show where the train was.'

Elwyn sighed. 'Yes, there's all sorts of gadgets. Those track circuit repeaters came here in 1947 when they did away with the "Vehicle on Line" switches. I think they interlocked our starting signals with the "Line Clear" position on the block indicators at the same time. New-fangled stuff,' he growled, thumbing his snuff box up from its pocket. 'You'd think they'd trust us to get the "Line Clear" before we pulled off, wouldn't you?' I felt puzzled by this.

'Are you saying that you used to be able to pull the signal controlling the entrance to the next section *without* getting the road first?'

'Indeed you could – at hundreds of boxes and there are still plenty today where you could pull the starter off without "Line Clear" being up in the indicator. There was no such thing, in GWR days, as a white stripe on a lever to show that you had to get "Line Clear" before you could pull it; that only came in with BR.'

'What about these "Vehicle on Line" switches. Did they do the same job as the track circuit?'

'Oh yes, when the Up or Down switch was turned, you couldn't give "Line Clear" to the box to the rear – Challow on the Down and Knighton on the Up. The difference now is that the presence of a wagon on the line triggers the gadget. There's a current in each rail and the wagon's wheels bridge them and make a short-circuit and that works the locks and makes the indicator in the box show that you've a train standing "on the track".'

'The instrument shelf is very simple, isn't it? I mean, there's only a few signal and lamp repeaters and you haven't got a repeater for the water tank but there is one at Wantage Road.' I was, in truth, a bit disappointed, because Uffington looked such a simple box without rows of flashy instruments.

'Damn good job too!' said Elwyn. 'A signalman don't need 'em. All this locking – they really were signalmen years ago when they didn't have all this protection and had to keep their minds on the job. Old Sid Phillips, down at Ashbury, told me once that the old M&SW* boxes were hardly locked at all, you could have the distant "off" and all the stop signals "on" – dhu-man, you had to be a signalman in a box like that!'

'Do you believe that? Surely it can't be true?' I was quite incredulous. 'Well, old Sid said it was so. You ought to go and see him, nice old boy, he'd tell you a thing or two.'

'I've just thought – where is the pump-house for filling the water-tower?'

'There is no need of one. Those old engineers were clever men indeed. The water is brought from a well sunk up in the hills yonder. It's about a hundred feet above the tank and just runs down here through a pipe – simple, see. And that's probably

---

* The Midland & South Western Junction Railway which ran from Cheltenham to Andover. Absorbed into the Great Western Railway in 1921.

why we've no "High" and "Low" warning instrument because there's no pump to go wrong so the tank never empties.'

'But how is it prevented from overflowing with that weight of water standing in the pipe? I'd like to go up to see the valve. It must be a huge ball and arm. Have you ever seen it?'

Elwyn made his disdainful face and reached for his snuff tin. 'Catch me climbing up water-towers – but I do know it's only broken down once in living memory – that was through abuse. I don't suppose you've met Walt Thomas – he was in the box here for thirty-seven years, retired when the passengers finished on the branch – he said it was a sleeve-valve – whatever *that* might be. He knew because a man servicing it one day wanted to see if it was working properly. He shoved the arm down and in came the water – lets go of the arm, the water cuts off. He was quite pleased with that, so he tried it two or three times more and then climbed down the ladder. When he got below the tank, he could see down the branch and saw a great fountain of water coming up from the ballast. Starting and stopping tons of water he'd put terrible pressures inside the pipe and it'd burst. There was hell to pot!'

The trains were passing all the while and minute by minute I wrote off the advancing morning – a signalman's job was the greatest 'clock-watching' occupation in the world – until it was one o'clock. 'Well now,' said Elwyn, rising from the armchair, 'I'll just visit the little 'ouse and then get round with the broom.' He went into the cardboard-walled lavatory, the cistern flushed and he emerged. 'Flimsy old place, that is. On engineering Sundays, when you've got a lot of men in the box, there's some who are embarrassed to use it and go down to the station u-*ri*-nals. Well, look you, go now, I can finish. Get here about seven tomorrow morning. No need to be dead on time. We'll do some more and maybe get the rule book out.'

I said my 'good-day' and drove home, very happy after a pleasant morning at work.

Chapter Twelve

A Duke at Breakfast

Elwyn was responsible for the safe working of the signal box and was liable to answer for any accident or delay to a train resulting from a mistake of mine. Over the next three or four weeks he let me work the box continuously while he talked about the rules and regulations or his own career, or other men's, with great cheerfulness so that I learned, simultaneously, my tangible work and the spirit in which it ought to be carried out. Nowadays, the NUR would like men to receive extra pay for this work but no one, then, considered such a thing. Elwyn taught me in the best tradition of 'fraternity', which the Union likes to think of as its own – no extra money would have made him any better at his job, but we each gained a friend.

Uffington was for the most part simply a 'passing' box, a larger edition of Lockinge but became more interesting at eight o'clock each morning when the 7.25 Swindon to Faringdon goods arrived; on Mondays and alternate weekdays it was joined by the Didcot to Uffington Fly and then the signal box was as busy as it ever had been.

The 7.25 Swindon was hauled by a pannier tank as a rule and on arrival at Uffington backed into the sidings through points 33. Considerable shunting and lever pulling ensued. The wagons for Uffington and local stations to Didcot were detached and the engine and brake van had to change ends of the train for the run to Faringdon. If the Fly was at the station, it would go up into Baulking sidings, clear of the Faringdon's manoeuvres; its crew having breakfast of tea and sandwiches, occasionally frying bacon and egg in the firing shovel placed just inside the furnace.

When the Faringdon had rearranged its train and taken water from the platform column, it would be standing quietly alongside the branch platform, the engine just outside the box and the driver, fireman or both men would come to the box for the 'train staff'. This was a piece of polished oak, triangular in section, about fourteen inches long, with an engraved brass plate UFFINGTON – FARINGDON. No driver could take his train onto the branch without the staff, and as there was only one, we avoided head-on collisions on the single line, without any more sophisticated system of signalling.

The driver came up into the box one morning soon after I started learning.

'Mornin' Elwyn, got a strapper then?' Elwyn introduced me.

'Can anyone tell me why a learner is a strapper?' I asked.

'No offence, mate,' said the driver, 'it's just a saying, never thought much about it. I reckon it must be as old as the railway; come to think of it, I was a "strapper" when I left school and went on the farm about 1920.'

'Have you worked over the branch a lot?' I asked next. The driver laughed.

'Me and old Sid Wilcox worked it in passenger days, didn't we, Elwyn?'

'Indeed, yes. Do you remember the time you lost old Sid's breakfast for him.'

'Oh ah! That was the day he chased me round the station with the shovel and the train was late leaving.'

'What was that then?' I looked from one to the other. Elwyn started to explain.

'They used to come up on a goods from Swindon and when they'd sorted out the shunting they went onto the coaches stabled on the run-round loop, hooked on and came into the platform ready for the day's service. So now they got onto the coaches but they were in plenty of time and didn't hook on.'

'No,' continued the driver, 'came up here for some fresh water to make Sid and me some tea – you must have only just come here then Elwyn – and when I got back to the engine old Sid was squatting down in front of the fire with some sausages frying in the shovel.'

'Then old Freddie Hands the guard came up,' Elwyn took up the tale, 'and says "Ease-up" 'cos he was going to go underneath and couple up, so Bert here' – I looked at Bert who was grinning all over his face – 'leans over Sid down by the fire and yanks up the regulator. "Whoof" goes the engine and, of course, the blast out of the chimney sucked the sausages off the shovel.' They both laughed at the memory and Bert continued.

'Old Sid was furious 'cos he'd lost his grub and come at me wi' the shovel. I jumped off the engine and ran and him following – he stepped on two of his blessed sausages!'

'You see,' said Elwyn, 'they'd been blown out of the chimney; I saw them come out of the funnel – I was trying to tell them but I was laughing too much to shout properly.' He shook his head slowly, 'D'you-mon, what a morning!'

Just then the guard came in. 'Come on then, how about a bit of railway work – mornin' Elwyn. Oh! Got a mate?' I was introduced again. 'Come on then, Bert, let's get off.' They went down the steps, climbed aboard their respective parts of the train and with a cheerful 'toot' the train left. So much for the rules governing the working of the branch.

'When did you come to Uffington, Elwyn?' I asked after the train had gone.

'January 1943. Fred Joyce and Walt Thomas were here then, steady old boys they were, old Fred was a bit crusty at times – huh! He started on the railway at Highclere in 1899 and came here in 1910 so I suppose he was entitled to get a bit short tempered now and then.'

'Where did Walt Thomas start?'

'Up at Paddington in 1902. I learnt the job from him so we spent some time together and I know a bit more about his life. He was a signal-porter at Marlow, a signalman at Greenford, then at Shrivenham and came to Uffington in 1914 – he retired only ten years ago. You could go and see him, he's always out in his garden by the main street of the village. Him and Fred were very close friends; them and two other chaps clubbed together, bought an acre of land from the Craven estate and had two semi-detached houses built. Very solid jobs they are – Fred and Walt still live side by side with their families.'

'They must have been very well paid to have afforded all that.'

'Well, I don't know about that. Better paid than any other worker locally. Railway wages were high forty years ago compared to most working-class jobs, and what was just as important, you knew you wouldn't be laid off. A porter would have to move for promotion or because the Company decided he wasn't needed where he was – but they didn't sack him, and once he became a signalman at a reasonably high-class box like this, he knew he was set for life with a regular job – so he could have raised a mortgage, I suppose.'

'Was the branch very busy when you got here, Elwyn?'

'Not as busy as it had been in the '20s – Walt said they had twenty-two trains a day then – but busy enough all the same. We had two passenger trains booked each way morning and evening and at least one extra trip each way with loaded and empty siphons and tanker wagons of milk.'

'They used milk *tankers*?!'

'Indeed, yes. It was the war, petrol shortage, they had to put all the milk back on rail. Literally millions of gallons of milk came up the branch for London. The biggest engine they could use was a "Spinning Jenny", so they often went double-headed to cope with the overload.'

'What was a "Spinning Jenny"?'

'Oh, I don't know. A little tender engine, six-coupled with a big dome. They used to bring the milk up to here and leave it for the Chippenham to collect. In the evening you'd have a pair of them waiting just outside for the Wood Lane to drop the empties off and then they'd work it all down to Faringdon. Them days you used the "Warning" – it's still on the extra rules for the box but we never have to use it nowadays.'

Normally a signalman was forbidden to give 'Line Clear' for a train to approach unless the line on which the train was to run was clear for at least a quarter of a mile beyond the home signal. The spot where the quarter-mile distance ended was known as the 'clearing point' and signalmen made a mental note of some landmark to show them this important place. Elwyn pointed them out to me; they were not very conspicuous. 'On the Up road the clearing point falls eighty yards short of the advanced starter, so we use the signal as the marker to have something definite and on the Down road we reckon the road over-bridge marks the spot.'

The bell code for giving the 'Warning' was 3-5-5, which seemed exotic and I looked for an excuse to use it. One day, while I was still learning, the engine of the Fly wanted to take water. The Faringdon goods was blocking access to the water column at the branch platform so the engine had to come onto the main line to stand by the column and was then well inside the clearing point.

Knighton Crossing then asked 'Line Clear' for a 'light engine' – an engine without a train – and I was delighted to be able to tap out the 3-5-5 code for the 'Warning Acceptance, Section clear but station or junction blocked'. There was a pause from Knighton until the penny dropped; obviously the code was hardly ever used, then back came the acknowledgement and in return I turned the block indicator to 'Line Clear'.

'That's very good,' said Elwyn, 'but do you know what you would have done in this case if you were *not* allowed to use the "Warning"?' I had not thought of that of course and groped around for a moment. 'Ah! I'd have had to "block back" with 2-4 on the bell before I let the engine out onto the running line.'

'And then what?'

'Well, Knighton would acknowledge the code if it was safe for him to do so and then I could have turned the block indicator to "Train on Line" and let the engine out.'

'How would you have cleared the block afterwards?'

'When the engine had gone into the siding and the points were set for main line running, I'd have sent "Obstruction Removed" – 2-1, the same code as "Train out of Section" and turned the block indicator to "Normal".'

'Right, you've got that. Now, what is Knighton Crossing doing with the engine you accepted under the "Warning"?'

'He'll bring it nearly to a stand at his home signal, lower it, and as the engine comes to the box, he'll hang a green flag from the window. The driver will acknowledge the flag with a toot on the whistle and then Knighton can pull off his starter because the driver knows that the line immediately ahead of the home signal is blocked.

'That's a piece of very old working, you know,' Elwyn said. 'An old railwayman I knew at Yeovil told me he'd started on the Great Western in 1884 when white was the colour for "All Right" and green was the colour for "Caution"; he reckoned it'd been changed around 1895 and gave me a little rhyme for the old rule:

White is right
And red is wrong
Green means gently go along.

'Can you tell me,' he went on, 'what you would do if the engine driver did not acknowledge the green flag but just went past as if he hadn't seen it?'

'I'd bring him to a stand at the starting signal and then immediately lower it but that doesn't seem very good to me; how can you be sure the driver knows what you mean?'

'Well, it's hope you must have, he'll have read the Rule Book and number 41 is written down specifically for that situation; does that reassure you?'

'Yes, I think it does. I'll have a look at rule 41, thanks.'

While we had been talking, Elwyn had been sitting in his chair and I had been watching the fireman of the Fly engine. He was standing on top of the engine's boiler, his back to me and Knighton, leaning against the arm of the column, engrossed in the sight of water swirling into the 1,200-gallon tanks. Only when the engine was quite close did he hear its sound. His head snapped round, and there was another engine approaching on the same track about 150 yards away. Knowing nothing of special bell codes and thinking that a crash was imminent, he took fright and jumped from the top of the engine to the platform with such abandon that he positively *bounced* off the paving, and with that momentum to help him came shooting up the short flight of steps and burst into the box – '*Look out!*'

Elwyn, who had seen none of this, leaped out of his chair and the fireman, leaning out of the box window, said, 'Thank God. It's stopped. What's your bloody game then mate?' I explained the situation to him and he went out, shaken but consoled to turn the tap off because his tanks were gushing water all over the platform. Elwyn settled back into his chair with a little laugh and snuffed himself. 'I reckon you're the first man to use the "Warning" here for years, causing chaos you are.'

'Well, what would you have done in the circumstances?'

'D'you-mon,' he said, drawing down the corners of his mouth, 'I wouldn't be so keen – I'd have asked the Faringdon to move back a few yards to make room for the Fly.'

Shunting the Fly and the Faringdon and fitting them into the traffic flow was the only 'regulating' duty we had. The Fly needed eight minutes to run up to Challow but the Faringdon returning to Swindon was a little more difficult.

Sometimes the porter at Faringdon would telephone to say when the goods had left but very often the first we knew of it was when we heard its whistle blowing loud and long, as it came galloping down the hill, for the branch home signal to be lowered. It arrived with the engine at the east end of the train and the guard's van at the west end so that, yet again, their positions had to be reversed before the train could leave for home. When the train was rearranged, the fireman would fill the locomotive's water-tanks while the driver came to the box with two conical drinking-water cans to be filled for Knighton Crossing, that box's only supply. The full cans were placed on the buffer beam of the engine, which then backed the train up into Baulking sidings to await a path across the Up main, to the Down main for the west-bound run.

Two minutes were needed for it to clear the Up main. If an Up or Down train was 'asked' while the train was crossing over, I simply 'refused the road' – that is, I did not acknowledge the bell code until such time as the points were set for the main lines and the clearing point was clear; there was no sense in using the 'Warning' for so temporary a block. Once on the Down main I allowed the train eighteen minutes to stop at Knighton, restart and get into the goods loop, clear of the mainline, at Ashbury.

As the Faringdon was leaving for Swindon one morning, Elwyn was leaning from the window at one end of the box and I was leaning out of the other. We watched the train out of sight and stayed leaning on the bar enjoying the sun and the quiet. A pair of rooks in sober black with grey beaks like pickaxes were strolling along the crown of a rail, stopping now and then to peck or look at something.

'D'you see th' old gangers?' said Elwyn. I looked for some men and Elwyn, seeing me puzzled, said, 'The old rooks there. Don't you know they are the ghosts of long-dead gangers? That's why they're always patrolling the track – if they find a piece of ballast lying on the rail, they'll throw it off.' I looked uncertain but he pressed his point, 'I knew an old ganger who said he depended on the rooks to show him the hanging joints – where there's a cavity beneath the sleepers at a joint between rails – he swore that the rooks left a piece of stone on the sleeper of a bad joint.'

A bell rang and we went in. Knighton was asking the road for the 7.30 Carmarthen, the Up Red Dragon; I answered it while Elwyn put the kettle on. He went to the window sill and sat in the sun and I sat on the coal box, by the door and the back window. 'Where were you before you came here, Elwyn?' He thumbed up his snuff tin and offered it to me.

'No thanks very much.'

'I came out of school in 1929 at Bridgend – handy place to be that year too. I didn't have a proper job for five years but I'd had my name down with the Great Western and in the end I got a note from them – I could have a class 2 porter's job at Sparkford. Didn't know where it was, Somerset they said. Well, I was so pleased at having a proper job and on the railway that I took it and went. I'd hardly got there when they decided the place was overstaffed and sent me to Yeovil Pen Mill, same grade.'

'I've never been down that part of the world; what was it like?'

'Oh! Somerset is a beautiful place, though you, coming from round here, might not appreciate it as much as I did, coming up from Glamorganshire and the pits. Yeovil had a queer layout indeed. There were three stations there – Pen Mill was on the Great Western line from Castle Cary to Weymouth and had a branch going round to the Town station half a mile away, that was a joint station with the Southern and then there was the Southern station proper, Yeovil Junction, up on the Waterloo–Exeter line which crossed over the Weymouth line about a mile and a half south of Pen Mill. There was a fine, deep cutting between Pen Mill and the Southern main line and the tracks were four abreast for a while, two of ours and two of theirs and then theirs went up a steep bank to join the Exeter road.'

'And did you have a junction between the Southern and the Great Western on the four-track section?'

'No – Ha! T'wud have been a good idea if there had been. In fact I believe they did lay something in during the war for the ambulance trains – and built a big, new signal box too – but when I was there in 1934, anything for the Southern had to be humped out of one train and into another just as if we had a break of gauge. That was what they wanted me for at Yeovil, humping parcels and people out of the Weymouth trains and into the little dasher that went round to the Town station.'

'Was the Town station a terminus then, served by an engine and coach?'

'Bless you no! The line went through to Taunton and we got Southern tankies coming into Pen Mill from the Junction via the Town. It was a queer place. People from Weymouth line stations for Exeter used to have to get out at the Great Western Pen Mill station, cross the platform for a dasher round to the town, get out again and get into a Southern dasher, go up to the Junction station, going back the way they'd come for a mile or so, get out of that train and wait on the platform for the express to Exeter. 'Course, if they got into a Southern dasher at Pen Mill, they didn't have to change at the Town.'

'I wish I could have seen it; it must have been marvellous to have both companies' engines working into your station and all that complicated railway.'

'Oh, it would have suited you all right, but I know the booking clerks used to get some tricky accounting when the passengers were booking through from a Great Western to a Southern station.'

'Were you there long?'

'Oh yes, four years. I applied for all the promotion I saw advertised and it took that long to get the service in to make a move beyond the bottom grade of porter. But it wasn't so bad. My wages were £2 a week, I had a good lodge, and for £1 my landlady gave me full board and did all my washing and ironing, and very clean and decent the house was indeed.'

The 1-2-1 code rang from Knighton. I answered it, 'got the road ahead' from Challow and pulled off. Elwyn came in from the sun and made the tea as the Challow bell 'dinged' one beat. I answered and got a 3-2 bell for a slow goods train.

'I went down to Portland, porter-signalman. I had from 2 p.m. to 4 p.m. in the box and the rest of the time I was humping sides of bacon in the goods shed – that and ingots of steel for Whitehead's torpedo factory. D'you-mon, it was murder, and when the Fleet was in – Oh! The sacks of brussels sprouts and kegs of rum.' Knighton rang the 'Train on Line'. 'I got out of that pretty fast. I was lucky, and landed the highest paid porter-signalman's job in the Bristol division – permanent early turn at Weymouth Town station. The box was a Class 2 and I worked it from 6 a.m. till 8 a.m. and then went up the station for portering. Till two o'clock.'

'When did you get your first signalman's job?'

'I went to Pilning Low Level in 1939. It was only Class 5 – but that was better than Class 6 and it shared in the Sunday work at Severn Tunnel East.' The Dragon came hammering through behind a 'King' class engine, I sent it 'on line' to Challow and received 'on line' for the 3-2 goods train at the same time. I 'got the road' from Knighton, put the Up signal to 'Danger' and then 'pulled off' on the Down road for the goods.

'I suppose you had to move though, for the promotion?'

'Well, that and the bombing.'

'*Bombing?*'

'Well, yes,' he took a sip of tea, 'we were in the middle of dockland there, Bristol, Avonmouth and Newport and then there was the Bristol aircraft factory at Filton.

Bloody Jerry was always over, sometimes just a "tip-an'-run" but very often a full-scale raid on somewhere; they had plenty to choose from,' his face suddenly became very indignant and he sat up straighter in his chair, 'and damn-all *sleep* could man get when *they* were buzzing around, dropping their bombs and our guns firing back.' He delved for his snuff.

'Well, I suppose it wasn't too difficult to find somewhere quieter with all the staff shortages that there were then?'

'Huh! I didn't get away until 1942 and then I went to Yarnbrook between Westbury and Trowbridge. It was only a break-section box like Lockinge but there was so much traffic that it was a Class 4 and after a year o' that I moved to here. It did Walt Thomas for thirty-seven years and I reckon it'll do me the same. That's the funny thing about Uffington; people come here from miles away and stay forever.'

The goods train came tonking under the bridge down in the cutting and I got up to see to it. The engine was a '63' class making about 30 mph. I watched from the open window as she came down towards the box snorting a brisk rhythm and her driver, leaning over the cab-side, looking at the ground, seemed to be listening to it intently. He looked up as he drew close to the box, I saw his hand reach for the whistle chain. The whistle 'pooped' twice and the engine passed the box with a wave and a smile from her driver. Her cab, unmodified after forty years, had very skimpy side-sheets; her tender was low. I had a perfect view into the cab: her fireman was busy with his coal-pick tugging coal forward on the tender; her fire, just visible behind the fire-hole flap, was pure, incandescent, white.

I put the signals back to 'Danger' and attended to the bells, passing them to the register. 'You really enjoy watching them engines, don't you?' said Elwyn, just a little amused.

'Yes, I always have done, I feel fond of them, the same feeling I had for the pony I used to ride before I left school, or perhaps even more than that. There's something about the rhythm they make and the way they seem to work for the driver. No wonder they were called the iron horse.'

'You'd have liked it here a few years ago when we had the Royal train to stable on the branch. It came two years running with the Duke of Edinburgh both times.'

'Did they take a main line express engine onto the branch?'

'Indeed, yes. A "Castle" it was and they had to take the coping stones off the milk dock or its cylinders would have struck against them on the sharp curve, even then it had a job to get round; I saw then why they don't let big engines on the branch, they nearly get wedged on the curve. If you go down the hill on the branch, you'll find the white post with a lamp bracket that was put up to mark where the driver had to stop – he had to have the lamp exactly between the engine and the tender and then he knew that the tail of the train was clear of points 30. Hah! I often wondered how the ol' Duke slept when the train was tilted on a 1 in 88 gradient. Ol' branch ganger had to crawl under the lavatory pipes with chamber pots – d'you-mon, he was Chairman of our branch of the Union too.

Those pots had the Royal Arms on them and in the morning he had to go in and fetch 'em, wash 'em out and put 'em onto the train.'

I laughed at this because I knew the man a little and could just imagine his indignation. 'He was more of a republican than ever after that, I suppose?'

'Republican, is it?' said Elwyn indignantly. 'He was livid!'

'Well, next morning I was having my egg and bread, about seven, when the door opens and who should walk in but the Duke of Edinburgh! There I was in my shirt sleeves and no collar, just like I am now. I got up – I didn't know whether to bow or what but before I'd sorted myself out he'd come over and shaken hands with me. Very nice chap, you know. I can say that too, as a life-long Labour voter. He wanted to know about the box and I told 'im and then I felt we were getting on fine so I offered 'im a cup of tea but he turned that down – said he had a breakfast waiting for him in the train – so he shook hands again and went out. Dear, dear, when I sat down – my breakfast was all cold. I nearly went to him for a bit of hot food.

'The amazing thing was that they stabled him on the branch the following year, police and soldiers all over the place, and blow me if I wasn't on early turn. Well, I sat down to my egg and tea about seven and I'd not taken the top off the eggs when the door opens and in he comes again. "*Oh drat!*" I thought, "another cold breakfast." But he said "Not still eating that egg?" and grinned, so I felt better; we shook hands – he's a great man for that – and I offered him a cup of tea and this old armchair so's I could get on with my breakfast.

'Well, he said that'd be all right and sat down but then I realised that my spare mug didn't have a handle. I tried the other chaps' lockers but they were both locked and there he was, waiting for his tea and my breakfast getting cold again. Dear, dear. So he had to have the handle-less mug but he minded less than me and must have sat, watching me work the box and talking for twenty minutes; I reckon he'd have liked to have had a go himself. Then he got up and said, "Thank you very much, Mr Richards"' – I broke in: 'And shook your hand again?' – 'Yes – shook 'ands and says "I'd better go and see what they've got me for breakfast." And off he went.'

'It must have been very fine to see a "Castle" pushing backwards off the branch and past the box into Baulking sidings and to see those beautiful coaches – I don't suppose anyone has a photograph of it?'

'No one but staff got anywhere near here, let me tell you. But it was a sight to see all right. They pushed down clear of the crossings, then I pulled off and that old engine came across to the down-side with a steady "one-two-three-four" out of the chimney.'

'Aha!' I butted in. 'So you see what I mean about the sort of music they play?'

'Well, I must admit they can look very good and sound good too, I'm very keen on music myself so I know what you mean. The last I saw of His Royal Highness was him waving to me out of his carriage as he passed the box. A very nice gentleman.'

Chapter Thirteen

Swindon Fashion

Remote though the setting of Uffington box was, Elwyn had several visitors, official and otherwise, to keep him company for a few minutes or two hours – even on the night shift. Mary, the wife of the Signal & Telegraph department technician who lived in the station house across the yard, came in for a few minutes each day when she brought the daily newspaper. She came originally from Somerset and her bright smile and cheerful West Country voice reminded me of cider apple orchards on a sunny day. Mr Halford came to the box when he visited the station but never stayed longer than he had to. The station's porter, Les, always came up for his afternoon tea and might spend the hour telling you about his infallible plan for robbing a bank or he might eat in silence except for clicking his biro point in and out – for an hour. One Swindon reliefman was said to have evicted him for this but Elwyn said, 'He's the porter and he can come up here if he likes, just ignore him when the mood takes him.' On late turn and nights, when the vicar of the parish visited the box and had a sort of 'behind the scenes' vestry meeting, I discovered that Elwyn's hobby was parish church matters; he was a church warden and choirmaster.

After the vicar had left, late one night, I said to Elwyn, inquisitively I must admit, 'You and the vicar get around the countryside a good deal, Elwyn.'

'He likes a good, comfortable pub, where there's a nice, quiet atmosphere, good food and well-kept beer – the Trout at Lechlade or the Trout at Godstow, then there's the White Hart at Wytham ... you ought to get out to them, you'd like it; old-fashioned, handsome houses in a good setting with fine service.'

'It sounds like a hobby – I've never thought of it.'

'Don't tell me you had five years in the Army and never went drinking?'

'Well, that's just it, I used to go *drinking* – and very uncomfortable it was too. Scrumpy at tuppence a pint down on the Barbican at Plymouth or brown ale up Union Street. I gave it up after a while and went out watching trains instead; it was more interesting. I never went into any pubs like you're describing.'

'Well, of course, you got to find the right ones. I suppose a bunch of squaddies don't care too much so long as it's beer.'

'Well, they weren't vicars and choirmasters so they weren't looking for anything very profound – not up Union Street, anyhow. I must say, the way you describe it, it makes it sound like a very civilised form of entertainment. Do you go far afield searching for new places?'

'I make a weekend in London now and then – when I go up for my snuff and stop in some nice old place.'

'To London for snuff? Is there a great difference to the snuff you could get in Oxford?'

'Yes, probably, but it's not just that, it makes an excuse for a weekend away. I go to Fribourg & Treyer, near Leicester Square, for the snuff. It's a beautiful little shop. The firm have been there since 1720; it's still got its curved windows with small panes on each side of the front door – and brass window sills too. Inside they've got snuff in every scent you could wish for, they've got every kind of cigar, cigarette and pipe and it's all in eighteenth-century boxes and cupboards. The place is well worth going to just to look at and once you've been there a few times they know you and what you like so you have good service. Oh, it's very pleasant.'

'Yes, I see what you mean. It'd never crossed my mind. I went from school to the army and there tobacco meant "Woodbines" from the NAAFI and beer was whenever and wherever you could get it.'

'Once a year we have to take the choirboys for their outing to London. We go up on the nine o'clock from Challow and walk all round town from the Tower to Madame Tussauds with a lunch break at the George in Southwark – a beautiful place that. By the time we get 'em back to Paddington for the 5.5 they're so tired they go to sleep on the platform seats. We have to carry some of them into the train, but then we can get a few pints in the restaurant car to revive ourselves, me and the vicar, after our exhausting day shepherding them round, without worrying that they might be getting into mischief.' He said that with a deadpan face but with a gentle irony in his voice and I began to realise that Elwyn was quite a character.

I had worked with him for three shifts – early, nights and late – and felt fairly confident of facing the District Inspector and passing the rules examination. 'What's Mr Millsom like on the rules, Elwyn?' I asked on Monday morning of my fourth week learning.

'Oh, very fair. He'll ask you direct questions, nothing hidden or awkwardly put; he won't be trying to trip you up – very fair.'

'Well, thank goodness for that. Where's he from, do you know?'

'He started on the Berks & Hants line, Newbury, I think, as a booking lad. Jack Lockett was a booking boy, too, from Westbury and I think you'll find that the Chief Inspector at Bristol, Dick Wellman, comes from Westbury, too, or around there. Him and Albert Stanley were porters together.'

Later that morning Mr Millsom and Mr Lockett got off the Up stopper. 'Hey up, Adrian,' said Elwyn in the same hushed voice that I had heard Sam use at Challow, 'here they are.'

I knew from his voice who 'they' were and my stomach skipped up and down nervously. I watched them come along the platform. They made a splendid sight in their dark-blue, Melton-cloth overcoats and brown trilby hats. Mr Lockett a head taller than his colleague Mr Millsom, silver-haired, walking with his shoulders hunched, hands deep in his overcoat pockets, his head thrust forward, a briar pipe smoking thickly. Both men moved in a calm, self-possessed way – they were railway officers.

They came into the box. 'Mornings' were exchanged all round.

'Well, Elwyn, what do you think of your learner? Is he ready to take charge?'

'Oh yes, Mr Millsom,' said Elwyn loyally, 'I think he is.'

'What do you think, young man? Could you pass me on the rules?' He looked at me very hard, his bright-blue eyes keen under the dark brim of his trilby. I felt that it would sound horribly boastful to answer a simple 'Yes' to that question and instead said, 'Er, perhaps after a few more days, Mr Millsom.'

'Jack,' said the District Inspector, 'take him outside for twenty minutes on the rules.'

Mr Lockett was an older man than Mr Millsom and he had brown eyes that could never look anything but friendly. 'Come on then, Adrian,' he said, holding the door open for me. We strolled along the platform. 'Now don't worry about answering, you'll know the answer just by hearing the questions. Have you been working on the rules with Elwyn?'

'Yes, quite a lot.'

'Well then, you ought to be all right so long as you don't get excited about things.' He asked me a few questions about the rules as they applied to the station, standing at the west end of the platform and pointing out the places on the track where supposed failures or accidents had taken place. He was very gentle and I soon relaxed; it was like talking to Elwyn. 'You'll do,' he said after a while, 'we'll go back to the box.'

Elwyn and Mr Millsom were sitting, each with a mug of tea when we got back. 'There's fresh tea in the pot. Mr Lockett, Adrian, help yourselves.' I went to pour some tea but Jack Lockett waved me away. 'Sit down, I'll fetch it.'

'Well, what do you think, Jack? Will he do?'

'Yes, he'll be all right. You can have him down next week.'

'Right then, be in my office this day week at nine o'clock sharp,' said Mr Millsom emphasising the words by stabbing the air with the stem of his pipe.

After they had gone, Elwyn said, 'Right then, you'd better give me the duster – set to with the black Rule Book and the "Apple Green" signalling regulations. I'll give you a test each day.' I was certain of knowing Regulations 1 to 11 as they covered daily signalling routine and concentrated my efforts on the emergency codes in the latter part of the book.

Regulation 12 described the working of 'Obstruction Danger', 6 bells. This was rung to the box in the rear 'to prevent the approach of a train in the event of an accident, obstruction or other exceptional cause'. Regulation 13 concerned 'Animals on the Line' and how to deal with such trespass – curiously, no bell code was prescribed for this eventuality, neither did the book recommend that 6 bells should be sent for a herd of cows on the line. Regulation 15 gave instructions for

'Examination of the Line' under every conceivable circumstance; 14 told me how to remove a train from the section when its locomotive had failed; 16 advised what steps to take if a train was an unusually long time in the section; and 17 was 'Stop and Examine', 7 bells.

This commenced: 'Signalmen must be careful to notice each train to ascertain whether there is any apparent necessity for having it stopped at the next signal box for examination. If a signalman observes, or becomes aware of, anything unusual in a train such as signals of alarm, goods falling off, a vehicle on fire, hot axle box or other mishap – except tail lamp out or missing – he must send the "Stop and Examine" signal to the signal box in advance.'

Probably the commonest source of 7 bells was doors open on passenger trains or handles not properly turned. The signal was also sent for 'whistling noises', 'funny rattles' and 'bumping noises', literally anything that was, to the careful signalman, unusual. All signalmen felt they had a serious duty to investigate anything out of the ordinary, because if some small thing was let to go unchecked and subsequently caused an accident, the erring signalman would have to bear the omission on his conscience for a very long time. 17 was the Regulation of Absolute Care but its importance has lessened under the automatic system of signalling, which covers a large part of Western Region today because there are few places where a signalman can observe the trains.

Regulation 19 dealt with tail lamps. If a train passed a signal box and the signalman was uncertain whether the last vehicle was carrying its lamp, he had to assume that it was not, that the vehicle had broken away and was behind in the section. He would then send 9 bells to the box in advance and 4-5 bells to the box in the rear. The man receiving the 9 would stop the train for examination and the man receiving 4-5 prevented anything else from entering the section until it was known to be clear.

So they went on, through Regulation 20 'Train Divided' (accidentally) with the bell code 5-5, 'Train Running away in the Right Direction' 4-5-5 and in the 'Wrong Direction' 2-5-5, through 'Time Interval Working' when all the block instruments had failed, reducing everything to mere guesswork, to the final solution – 'Switching out Signal Box' aptly placed at the end of the book. Elwyn coached me through all this and far more, making tea, thinking up questions to ask – which, I found out later when I had to do it myself, is almost as hard as answering them – until on Friday he pronounced me well and truly crammed.

Next Monday I caught the 8.15 a.m. from Challow, boarding the train with a slap on the back and good luck wishes from Sam Loder. I travelled down with the three girls and would have been very happy with their company under normal circumstances but on that occasion I could barely speak. 'You're very talkative today,' said Veronica. 'Ugh! Sorry, I'm going for an examination on the rules and regulations so's I can be a signalman and I don't feel very well.' We got to Swindon at 8.45 and they left me with cheerful 'Good lucks' and, 'Tell us how you got on tomorrow.'

There was plenty to see on the station but it was hardly enough to take my mind off the dreaded interview. I strolled along the platform towards the West signal box, trying to think of some facts, and, being unable to recall any, feeling sick. Spare screw couplings and steam heating pipes hung on racks against the old, flaking stone walls of the station and in the centre of the platform stood a drinking-water tank on wheels with a tall pipe supporting a long, rubber hose for filling the tanks of restaurant cars. Across the branch track and a couple of sidings, against the wall that bordered the main road, stood the grounded body of an ancient coach. A pannier tank was shunting in the sidings by the West box and a grimy '63' class 2-6-0 was standing at the head of three coaches in the Marlborough Bay.

Beyond the big West signal box with its clock on the rear wall and the four-post bracket signal close by, I could see a brilliantly white plume of steam rising from an engine in one of the factory sidings down by Rodbourne Lane signal box – from one box to the next, locomotives lined the upside of the line waiting to go into the factory for repair. In the 'V' of the junction between the Bristol and Gloucester roads stood the tall building housing the Chief Mechanical Engineer's offices, including the locomotive drawing office of the Great Western Railway; in the sidings in front of the building, a steam crane was working, and opposite the West box, across a dozen tracks, a pannier tank was shunting in and out of the General Stores enclosure. The station announcer began to introduce the 7.30 a.m. Paddington, and the clock on the West box said five to nine – it was time for me to take the plunge.

Mr Millsom's office was in a limestone-faced building which stood above the street entrance to the booking office and appeared to be part of the original (1840) Brunel station and had probably been the District Inspector's office since signalling was done by lineside policemen in 1840. I crossed the tracks from the branch platform to a flight of stone steps which led to a double door opening into a corridor. I pushed through, heart beating fast, and saw DISTRICT INSPECTOR in gold leaf over cracked, brown paint. I knocked. 'Come in.' Turning the ceramic handle, I opened the door and walked in.

Mr Millsom was sitting behind a wide, leather-topped desk of late-Victorian design and of Swindon carriage works manufacture; indeed, there was hardly an item of furniture in the room that was not made in the railway factory. On the desk was an 18-inch boxwood ruler engraved GWR and a pair of rectangular, cast-iron paperweights also marked GWR. On one wall, between some Swindon-built cupboards, was a Great Western Railway coloured print from the 1890s showing a Dean '7-foot Single' – *John G Griffiths*. It was a famous picture, a broadside view of the engine at speed, the background blurred and the exhaust streaming back stiffly over the train. An ivory plate on the picture frame gave the title – *80 on the Flat*. On another wall was a coloured print from the late 1920s showing a 'King' hauling the Cornish Riviera Express out of Parson & Clerk tunnel onto the sea wall at Teignmouth, under the red cliffs of Devon. The carpet I was standing on had a blue, grey, yellow and black pattern into which was woven – yes, GWR!

Time was frozen for an instant in that office, it was 1931, not 1961 and *John G Griffiths* steamed on eternally across the wall – through time at '80 on the Flat'.

These pictures, which were then to be found in waiting rooms and offices all over the ex-Great Western Railway's territory, were, I think, taken for granted, hardly noticed but everyone felt it was right and proper that they should be there – they were part of the scene, part of the very mentality of railwaymen then and in that office they completed the atmosphere, leaving me without a shadow of doubt that, if I did not come up to the old Company's standards, I was not going to pass the examination. The Great Western Railway might have been physically abolished but before me was a man who still carried its standards high.

Mr Millsom waved me to a chair. 'Morning, Adrian, I hope you had a good night's sleep!' He picked up his pipe, started to pack it with a fresh charge of tobacco while I gripped my sweaty hands between my knees, and asked, 'If the wind blew the arm off a signal, how would you know what sort of signal the post should carry?' He worked away at his pipe. This was, literally, a stunning start. I was absolutely full of rules and absolutely nowhere is there any mention of such a thing. I thought of Elwyn's assessment that Millsom was a 'very fair man' and wondered just how much Elwyn knew about it.

Mr Millsom looked at me from the cover of a freshly lit pipe, his eyes shining through like stars on a cloudy night. With sudden relief I realised he was having me on and I remembered that stop signals have a red ball to their finial and distant signals have a yellow ball – something not mentioned anywhere in the rules or regulations but in fact quite an important point for an engine driver to know should he ever find a signal post minus its arm.

He laughed when I answered. 'There, that had you worried for a minute; now then, let's get on with the quiz.' The ice had been broken very cleverly by this excellent man and we set off on a four-hour session of question and answer. Occasionally he stopped to illustrate the regulation with interesting stories, one of which I remember clearly.

He had asked me when the 'Warning Arrangement' was employed at Uffington and what was the bell code for it. I told him and then he said, 'Down at Bincombe Tunnel box they were allowed to use the "Warning" if any train was "asked" while they were crossing the banker over to go back to Weymouth. There was an old chap there who'd worked the box for thirty years and the Inspector thought it was about time to give him a brush-up on the rules.

'He went along to the box and began asking the questions. The old chap got stuck almost straight away on Regulation 5 – he couldn't say what was the bell code for the "Warning". He had an Up train coming from Weymouth with a banker on behind and the Inspector was threatening to take him out of the box if he couldn't remember the code. Well, the Up train went by and the banker came to a stand by the box to cross over back to Weymouth and just as the cross-over was pulled, Dorchester "asked the road" for something and the old chap rattled out the 3-5-5, though it sounded more like a straight 13.

'"What's that you've just done?" says the Inspector.

'The old signalman looked guilty and nervous. "We always do that when the banker's crossing and we get one 'asked', Guv'nor."

'"But what do you *call* it?"

'"God bless my soul, Guv'nor, I don't know!"

'"*That is* the 'Warning' – you've just rung it!" It was a job to know who was the more surprised.'

I left Mr Millsom's office just after one o'clock, feeling as if I'd been squeezed through a mangle, but with an appointment to see the Chief Inspector and Divisional Superintendent at Bristol the following Monday.

The Chief Inspector, Dick Wellman, was a heavily built man, very down to earth and friendly. He spent a few minutes asking after Albert and Harry. 'I was at school with Albert, you know; either of them could have had this chair here if they'd cared to make all the moves for promotion but they settled down at Challow and never worried about it.'

'I spent some time with Harry and got the impression that what he didn't know wasn't worth knowing. He was quite formidable really – he's done most of the jobs in the Traffic Department, including the station master's, without moving out of the porter's grade.'

'Albert is just as capable. The old-hand porters had so much work to do, varied work, that they couldn't help learning a lot, from the sheer, physical hard work to the accountancy side – they had to know it all. And by the way you're wrong about Harry only ever being a porter; he was a Signalman at Circourt for a while. But did he ever tell you the work he had to do when he was a porter-signalman at Burbage Wharf?'

This seemed like the start of a good tale; at any rate, it was not 'rules'.

'Do you mean that old goods shed just south of Marlborough where the main road crosses the canal and the railway where they run parallel?' He seemed disappointed that I knew it.

'You know about it then?'

'No, not at all, except that I've passed over the bridge on my way home from Tidworth when I was in the Army and I often wondered what went on there. It looks as if it was an interchange between the canal and the railway.'

'Well, it might have been, long ago, but I don't think that's why it was put there. The town is only three miles away so the canal company built a wharf to serve it and when the railway came they built a siding and goods shed. I doubt that it was much of an interchange though, of course there was nothing to prevent it seeing as how the Great Western bought the canal people out.'

'It seems an out-of-the-way place to put a goods train. Was there much traffic there?'

'Ah, it does look like that now but when lorries weren't very reliable or plentiful it was very useful, right on the side of the main road and not too far from Marlborough. You got coal and farm machinery coming in, anything the district needed, and farm produce and cattle going out. On Marlborough fair days the big dealers would come down from London and Birmingham and they'd send cattle away from the Wharf, all over the country.'

'But what about the M&SW station at Marlborough; couldn't they have used that?'

'Well, of course they did – it was always very busy, especially on fair days, but it was only the station for some destinations.'

'So Harry was there all on his own, loading wagons, sheeting them, doing the paperwork and looking after the box?'

'Well now, I'm not sure about that, there may well have been one other man, simply doing portering. I don't know how the place was manned or what hours it opened to the public.'

'Did many trains call at the siding?'

'There were three trains booked to call in the mid-'20s, as I recall. The Reading to Bristol Fly was there from about half past seven to eight o'clock then they had the Up goods from Westbury to Ludgershall an hour later and the 5.15 Holt Junction to Didcot an hour after that.'

'Good Lord! You just wouldn't think that all those trains and all that work went on, looking at the place now.' My surprise was genuine. I found his revelations of this remote place very exciting and he was pleased with the effect they had had.

'Ah, and on top of that, Harry would have to arrange for special stops to be made by other goods trains to pick up consignments of cattle. The old farmers just turned up and dumped the animals and left us to find a service at the drop of a hat *and* feed and water their cows too – Harry'd have to see to all that. Another thing Harry was called upon to do was open the box to shorten the section. The box was three quarters of a mile west of Savernake West box and the line came up "in the collar" for sixteen miles from Lavington so when they had a few trains about, like on a summer Saturday, or if one was doing rough up the bank – and, of course, between Burbage and Savernake it was at its steepest bit – Harry would switch in to shorten the section between Savernake West and Pewsey.'

'That's absolutely fascinating – you go there now and it's still and quiet, nothing stirs, yet it was so busy a few years ago.'

Mr Wellman nodded happily. 'I'd heard you were interested in the old days – but this isn't what you're here for so let's talk about the General Appendix.'

He proceeded to ask me a lot of obscure questions from that obscure publication, none of which seemed to have any connection with the work at Uffington; none of which I could answer. 'That's the trouble nowadays,' he said, 'you blokes only read the bits that actually concern your job.'

But he said I'd passed and took me to see the Divisional Superintendent, Paul Pearman. He waved me into a beautiful, early-Victorian, mahogany chair with the letters B&ER (Bristol & Exeter Railway) carved in the backrest, asked me some questions on single-line working – which I answered – told me what *not* to do at Uffington, gave me a very old working timetable, told me that I was now a signalman, and suggested that I might like to visit the East signal box at Temple Meads. After the fatigue, the sweet – as the Duke of Cumberland once said.

Bristol Temple Meads East signal box was built in the severe style of the 1930s with a flat, concrete roof and red brick walls decorated by three strata of cement and all-round glazing in steel frames. A rectangular extrusion jutted out from ground to roof at the centre-front of the box to form a bay window in the operating room; the building was a huge box in more ways than one. It stood on the up-side of six or eight running lines midway between the station's fifteen platforms and its three geographical junctions, and from it all points and signals were controlled by electricity, the signals being colour lights.

I went in and climbed the stairs to the operating room where the three signalmen and their booking lad were expecting me. The latter was sitting in the bay window with his sleeves rolled up surrounded by a battery of telephones while the men were stationed in front of the longest row of 'levers' – small 'draw-out' handles, in fact – in the country.

The two furthest away kept their positions and waved a greeting and the man nearest the stairs said, 'It's Adrian, isn't it? Paul Pearman said you were on your way. The lad's put the kettle on so we'll all have one in a minute. Is Elwyn still at Uffington?' I told him he was. 'Good old Elwyn, steady as they come, great man for the Guinness.' I said I'd learnt Uffington under him. 'Then you're lucky – good company, good teacher. Tell him that Jessie Bye, Bill Barker and Fred Wilcox send their best wishes – we've all worked up through that part. Well now, Pearman told us to show you round – what do you think of our little toy?'

Bristol Temple Meads 'Old Station' looking from beneath the GW/Midland Joint station roof of 1876 to the original Brunellian terminal station of the Great Western Railway of 1840. I first saw this station when I went to Bristol for my examination on the signalling regulations by Chief Inspector Wellman and Divisional Superintendent Mr Pearman. Previously I had only seen the exaggerated scale of the Brunel station in the romaticised engravings of J. C. Bourne so seeing the station for real was something of a let-down. (Author)

After the fatigue, the sweet. After successfully completing my interrogation by Chief Inspector Wellman and then Divisional Superintendent, Paul Pearman, the latter gave me a fifteen-section GWR Working Time Table for 1936 – it weighs 5 lb – and suggested I visit Bristol Temple Meads East box. This was installed in 1934 and had 336 'draw slides' with which three signalmen controlled the electric light signals and electrically driven points to work the east end of the station and the tracks eastwards out to and including South Wales Junction. The signal box worked to the old 'Absolute Block' system. There were approximately twenty-three signalling bells and block instruments. All the bell codes received and sent were recorded by hand, on paper, by a teenage 'Booking Boy'. He also answered the telephones, and made enquiries on behalf of the signalmen. Signalmen Jesse Bye, on the left, and Bill Barker are shown. July 1961. (Author)

To work this place, the signalmen had to carry the entire timetable for Temple Meads station in their heads. (Author)

'I'm just overwhelmed – where do you start to look? I keep losing count of the number of block bells; how many draw-slides are there?'

'Walk along and count 'em,' he said with a grin. I paced perhaps twenty-five steps and counted twenty-two bells and 336 handles. 'What comes to my mind first is "How does your booking lad know which one is ringing?" Obviously he *does* but ...'

The booking lad grinned at me, 'You pick it up.'

'Why so many bells?' I asked him.

'Well, we're working with six signal boxes: Temple Meads West, Old Station, Goods Yard, Barrow Road, Doctor Day's and North Somerset Junction, and through the station, between the platforms, there's a dozen roads at least, each with a bell – it soon adds up.'

'How many boxes does all this replace?'

'Only two – the old East box that they called the "Coffin" box on account of its shape and South Wales Junction.'

'Are you sure it was the "Coffin" box only for its shape? It must have been a very heavy place to work with all the switching from platform to platform, shunting passenger stock and all on ordinary levers.'

'Well, this is all one handle to one point or one signal – not like the other Great Western power boxes where you set up a whole route, maybe a dozen points, with one lever. We've got all that fan of tracks going into the platforms or through the middle; then we've the junction to the Midland for Gloucester and Bath for the old Somerset & Dorset; in the middle we've got four tracks going round to Doctor Day's for South Wales or Paddington via Badminton or round to Avonmouth; then there's the old main line to Paddington through Bath and between those two routes you've got Doctor Day's carriage sidings.'

'Where's the tea? I think I'd better have a cup! I'd never be able to work this.'

'Ah you would; you'd pick it up,' said the booking lad modestly, pouring my tea with one hand and writing bell code times in the register with the other.

The signalmen set up serpentine routes, often in cooperation with each other, walking up and down their length pushing or pulling handles with a nonchalance that made them appear to be working at random. I could turn from watching the route being set up and look out over the orderly confusion of tracks and watch the trains that had just been signalled come past the box. 'Kings', 'Castles', 'Patriots' and 'Jubilees' slogging away from the station or freewheeling in, their trains following heavily, dun-dunning over the rail joints, flanges squealing against the curves. Names I recollect from that visit were those of the 'Devonian' express which left, northbound, double-headed behind a 'Patriot' 45509 (which ought to have been named 'Commando' but never received the plate) and 'Jubilee' 45577 *Bengal*. It was, without any doubt, the finest train set that I or anyone else will ever see.

I left the box after three hours, with many thanks to the four of them for their hospitality. I had, of course, enjoyed the visit but I did not feel I wanted to work there. Maybe it was too clever for me or perhaps it did not conform to my idea of a signal box; at any rate, I travelled home thrilled at the thought that I was a signalman and full of the anticipation of my first shift at Uffington on Monday morning.

Chapter Fourteen

Signalman's Morning

On Monday I woke to my alarm just after five o'clock. I felt as if it was my birthday and got out of bed immediately so as not to miss the party. Through the small window sunk deep in the thatch I saw the sun just above the horizon, shining promisingly through a few strands of night clouds. The village was silent in the bright light, not even a chimney smoked, the long grass in the meadow opposite seemed to be asleep, lying bent and flat under the weight of dew, and even the cows were lying down.

After a wash, some tea, bread and marmalade, I picked up the bag of sandwiches my mother had cut the previous evening. 'I shan't make them until the very last moment, so they'll be fresh,' she had said. I unbolted the back door and stepped outside into a cool, sunny morning. The sun was clear of the cloud now and as I walked across the garden to my car I could see in sharp detail every beech tree in a plantation on the ridge of the Downs over a mile away. The air was as clear as water in a stream, colours were bright and fresh. It was a signalman's morning, I thought, and felt happy.

I drove by way of Challow station so as to meet Bill Mattingley, who I knew would be coming from Uffington for early turn at the box and passed Jenny Carter trudging along the grass verge going to fetch her cows. At Challow the signals were 'off' for the York to Swindon passenger train and a goods waited patiently on the relief line for a 'path'. The signalman, waiting at his levers, saw me going over the bridge and waved – I blew a 'Victory V' on the horn. Two miles further on I met Bill, who was obviously looking out for me; we exchanged rude signs and triumphant smiles through our windscreens as we passed.

Crossing Baulking common, I saw Uffington's Down distant signal – *my* distant signal – the post and lowered arm brightly lit in the clear sun, white, yellow and black against the green backdrop of the Downs. At the bridge over the cutting I stopped briefly to look down on the station at the far end, the red-brick walls dark even in the morning sun but the box's faded cream paint blazing, almost white, between the green cutting sides. I felt so proud of it. My signal box!

The signals were pulled off in each direction because the box had been switched out of circuit since Saturday evening and I drove on rehearsing the procedure for switching in. I freewheeled down the sloping approach road to the station at ten to six; Pete's house curtained and still on my right; the single track of the Faringdon branch only a few feet away on my left, level with the road. The station was deserted and I walked along the platform, past the shuttered windows of the junction Hotel, feeling glad to be a part of the morning. Taking the signal box key from its hiding place, I went up the steps, opened the door and went inside.

The clatter of my shoes on the stairs, the clicking of the door lock as it opened and shut seemed like a great commotion in the bright silence of the box. I put my bag down on the coal bin and stood still, looking around, feeling the quiet, feeling as if the box was watching me, waiting to see what sort of signalman I should be. The sun came pouring through the east end windows, over my shoulders, flashing off silver block bells and the polished steel handles of the levers, brightening their red and yellow paint, leaving deep, chocolate-brown shadows and falling full on the face of the brass-cased clock at the far end of the room. After a few moments I could hear its busy ticking and the thoughtful call of a wood pigeon outside.

To find the place empty, the levers at each end of the frame pulled over, gave me an odd sensation; I was the on-duty officer, solely responsible for the safe running of the trains yet I was momentarily at a loss to know what to do and felt afraid to touch anything. I got in at the shallow end by signing on duty in the Book – 21 June 1961. A. Vaughan on duty 5.55 a.m. – and then set about the business of switching in.

I phoned Bill at Challow. 'Hi-up, Bill, what's about?' He roared back in exaggerated Berkshire, as he was liable to do when he was excited. ''Marnin' boy, 'Marnin' boy. You can come in. That thur goods went out behind the York and ain't gorn by Knighton yet so turn yer Down line block to "On Line". I dwun't suppose it's still between thee and I but just in case it is dwun't'ee put yer Down line boards back till you sees it go by or you get "Train Out" from Knighton. Thurs nothing on the Up.'

'Well I've got to phone Knighton so I'll ask the chap there if he can see the goods. Who's on there?'

'Old Tommy Morgan. Well, I'll hear from you later; give us a ring if you want anything.' His handset crashed down on its rest in true Mattingley style.

'Hello Knighton, Uffington here, I'm going to switch in. Can you see the goods on the Down road?' A rather frail, elderly voice came back. 'Hello. Is that Elwyn's learner? How's Elwyn this fine morning? I can see the Down goods.'

'Elwyn's on nights. This is Adrian, I've just taken on, this is my first shift.'

'Oh yes? Well, the very best of luck to you, young man; I hope you'll be happy there. Well, first of all, put your Down line indicator to "On Line", put all your levers back and send me the 5-5-5 on the bell.'

How careful they all are, I thought, as I turned the brass handle on the block switch. Using my left and right hands simultaneously, I tapped out the 'Opening of Signal Box' code to Challow and Knighton. The bells came crashing back, high and low pitch making a jangling discord together; Tommy's ringing taking several seconds longer than Bill's to finish.

A very far cry from Bristol Temple Meads East box, but, after many years of unofficial apprenticeship, I was thrilled to be a properly certified 'Officer in Charge' of Uffington box. (H. O. Vaughan, August 1961)

The Faringdon branch, 3 ½ miles long, swung sharply away to the north from Uffington station, and fell at 1 in 140 for half a mile over the Ock Brook and then rose up the Faringdon ridge at 1 in 88 for 1 ½ miles to the summit and thereafter gently fell and rose and levelled for the mile and a half into Faringdon. The steep fall out of the station followed by the long, steep rise gave ample opportunity for drivers to 'rush the bank' and see how many wagons they could get over the summit without stopping to divide the train. This view, looking to Faringdon, was taken from the lamp platform of the Up distant signal. The latter remained *in situ* for many years after the track had been lifted. (Author)

Faringdon station with its engine shed partly in view on the left and its goods shed on the right. (R. M. Casserley)

Faringdon yard in about 1958 with 0-4-2 tank No. 1410 shunting and the Oxford University Railway Society enjoying themselves. (Peter Barlow/Author's Collection)

No. 1410 on the
Faringdon–Uffington
trip with the branch
goods, pulls up the
grade towards the
summit of the line
c. 1958. (Peter
Barlow/Author's
Collection)

The Up branch home
signal at Uffington
in 1961. This was
the only semaphore
signal remaining at
the station for the
branch; there was
a couple of ground
discs too. The cast-
iron finial on top of
the post was of very
unusual design in that
the 'ball' was pierced
with a double row of
keyhole-shaped holes.
I have always thought
that this signal was
erected in 1896 when
the old signal box and
associated signalling
– Brunellian disc
& crossbars – were
abolished. A double
disc and crossbar
stood here in 1895.
(Author)

I put the kettle on for tea and walked across the box, looking out of all the windows, trying it for size – it seemed a different place now that I was on my own – wondering when a bell would ring. I got my first summons at 6.20 and thereafter the line was quite busy. Les the porter arrived at seven o'clock followed soon after by two regular passengers and at 7.15 the train for Reading pulled in behind an ex-works 'Hall' which came to a stand directly outside the box. I went to the window, of course, to admire *my* engine and *my* train.

The fireman was sitting, leaning over the cab-side, looking back for the guard's 'Right Away' and glanced up at me. 'All right then mate? How's Elwyn?' I told him I was on my own and he turned into the cab, apparently to pass this on to his driver just as the guard's whistle blew. The driver eased open the regulator and pulled down on both whistle chains. The deep, booming brake whistle and the high, clear 'every day' whistle merged into an ear-splitting howl; the engineman grinned and waved back over the coals as the train drew away and the guard, looking out, puzzled at the noise, saw me, understood and waved his greeting too. I realised I would never be absolutely alone when there were so many well-wishing workmates around.

The friendliness of the stopper's crew gave me an appetite for breakfast so I set water to boil for tea and for eggs (some men used to save electricity and boil their eggs in the tea water), laid bread on the table and as soon as the 5.30 Paddington to Plymouth fast had gone by sat down by a sunny window to eat.

A continuous tapping on glass made me look round several times, puzzled, till I saw a starling on the window sill asking to be fed. I got up to throw him a crust, as I did so the bells rang for the Paddington parcels and the Faringdon goods and thereafter breakfast was constantly interrupted by noisy trains and persistent birds so that the debris of the meal was still on the table when I went to the levers to shunt the Faringdon into the Up sidings.

The train arrived from Swindon behind 1644, one of the smallest pannier tanks in service, with sixteen coal-tubs of wet ashes for the town. It looked like an overload for the bank and I hoped that the crew would decide to split the load and make two trips.

The driver came up into the box for the Train Staff. 'Mornin', Bobby,'* he said cheerfully. 'On your own, now then? Still eating too, cor, it's a good life in the box, breakfast in peace sitting in the sun. Did Elwyn tell you about the mushrooms on the branch? They're all in a field on the right of the track just round the corner. Real beauties, too; we always pick some on this job when they're in season. They'd make your job sheer luxury.'

'I love mushrooms, especially fried in butter with fresh brown bread and butter.'

---

* Signalmen were often referred to as 'Bobbies' in recognition of the time between 1835 and 1875 when the trains were signalled by hand by constables patrolling the lineside.

'Aha! It's easy to see you'll be all right as a signalman – you're a born guzzler like the rest of them.'

'Huh! A lot of time we have for guzzling. I couldn't even eat a few bits of bread without interruption this morning – I even had a starling knocking on the window for food.'

'There you are – it was a signal box starling, greedy. Never mind, fatten it up and have in a pie with mushrooms in the autumn. Right, well I'm off, I'll see you later.'

'What about your train? It looks like an overload; are you going to make two trips?'

'No!' he said derisively. 'There'd be nothing in that. I'm going to take the whole load to see if she'll make it up the hill.'

He was, without doubt, a man after my own heart and I warmed to him. 'But what sort of tonnage have you got on? Those soggy ashes look heavy.'

He rubbed the back of his head and tipped his hat over his eyes. 'Ooh, it's a job to say. In fact you'll find that we're allowed nineteen wagons of coal up the hill with this engine which would be about 320 tons but that'd be as much as she'd ever take and our sixteen ashes feel a damn sight heavier than nineteen of coal!' He pushed his hat back into place decisively and reached for the door. 'Anyhow, we're going to have a go. My mate's got a big fire in and plenty of water. See you later.' He grinned at me and went out. The bus line telephone rang at that moment and I answered it. 'Uffington here.'

'Thompson here at Reading. Is Peter there please?' This was the Signal and Telegraph Inspector making his daily 7.30 a.m. call to ensure that Pete, our S&T technician, turned up for work on time but he would not have been in the department if he could not have rigged up a telephone circuit. He had laid one from his house to the signal box with a switch to enable it to be connected to the bus line circuit.

'Oh yes, Mr Thompson, you're only just in time; he's just off down the line. I'll go and shout to him,' I said, before turning the switch to speak privately to Peter.

'Reading on the line, Pete.'

After a decent interval I turned the switch once more and Peter – out of breath from running to greet his Inspector gasped, 'Hello, Mr Thompson …' Thus our technician could eat his breakfast when he should have been working and talk to his boss who had got out of bed early that morning and every morning to make the call. I put the phone down and went to the back window to see what the men on the Faringdon were doing.

They had backed their train up into the Baulking siding, 200 yards from the box, in order to have as great a distance as possible in which to work up speed for the climb of Barrowbush Hill, the little engine was blowing off steam in the cutting and then, with a long blast on her whistle, she took up the challenge and set out on the run.

There was no question of going easy – the engine was pulling for all she was worth from the start – but also, there was no danger of her speeding over the sidings and coming off the rails. She came blasting past the box, black smoke jetting from her chimney, wheels squealing on the rails, almost losing adhesion and spinning under the best efforts of the pistons' thrusts fed from a wide-open throttle. Driver and fireman shouted something and waved as they passed, the wagons followed sullen, wheels thudding dully over the rail joints.

The branch curved very sharply as it left the station, turning through 90 degrees from heading west to heading north, dropping into the valley of the Ock for nearly half a mile on a 1 in 140 gradient before crossing the stream and commencing the climb of Barrowbush Hill, rising at 1 in 140. Once the engine had squealed round the curve and tipped downhill, acceleration was rapid and as the guard's van swung round the bend the guard made 'hanging onto my hat' gestures to me watching from the signal box.

The sound of tearing exhaust came back clearly as the train gathered speed and I felt a sudden surge of excitement as an increase in its volume signalled that the driver had 'given her another notch'. This was not just bravado. Loose-coupled trains were curious things; the front part could be drawn along, couplings taut under the influence of the locomotive's pull while the rear half-dozen could be running with couplings slack and buffers jostling and this was even more likely on a steep downhill grade. When the gradient reversed the rear wagons would then, naturally, slow down while the front part drew away. Then the rear couplings chains would be drawn out tight – and with such a tug as might snap one of them. By putting on more steam the driver hoped to accelerate his train and draw out the slack in the rear couplings before the uphill stretch was reached.

1644 went ripping into the climb but with such a heavy train her exhaust beats began to slow almost at once, the driver, gave her yet another notch and she struggled on up the grade with a beat that might have been from a live animal, out of breath and over-burdened, till she crept over the summit with a gasping 'chuff' once a second from her chimney and so passed from earshot.

At a few minutes after eight o'clock the head of a laughing, chattering procession on bicycles could be heard in the lane, passing the Junction Hotel and seconds later the first of twenty-five girls for school, college and offices in Swindon arrived at the gate in the Down platform fence and wheeled her machine along to the down-side shelter. The rest, straggling in in small groups over the next five minutes, threw their bikes, clattering, into a pile against the shed wall.

It was a scene of pretty confusion as girls with bicycles walked to the shed and collided with girls walking from the shed to the footbridge. They trampled across the bridge's wooden boards to the Up platform, chattering like a flock of starlings, entered the booking hall and invaded the booking office. There, they issued their own tickets, date stamped them, put the fare in the till and took change while Les cowered in a corner. In fairness to him I must say that in a confined space they would have been formidable opponents, and in any case, Les cared only for the welfare of his flower beds, which had contributed much towards his third prize in the Bristol Division's 'Best Kept Station' competition in 1959.

Back at Uffington, No. 1410 must take water at the column, 'run round' the train *via* the branch loop and – after placing the refilled can of drinking water for Knighton Crossing signalman on the front buffer beam – 'push back' into Baulking sidings from whence to emerge for Swindon. (Peter Barlow/Author's Collection)

When the Swindon–Faringdon and the Didcot–Uffington goods trains were at Uffington, signalling became non-routine and much more initiative-led. The trains swapped wagons, the engines took water, the main line was required for shunting movements. Here the Didcot engine, 9754, is taking water on the main line before leaving for Challow. The Faringdon train waits on the branch while the crew are in the signal box making fresh tea. 1961. (Author)

No. 3818 passing Uffington with an 'F' headcode goods in January 1962 when the temperature by day was 15 degrees F below zero. (Author)

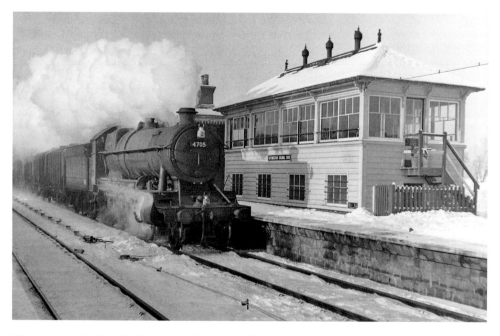

No. 4705 coming bravely through the Siberian cold with a very lowly 'H' headcode goods. I recollect that he was clipping along at a good speed – for a long, heavy freight and the driver clearly felt very confident of his massive engine's braking capability – the long train behind him being entirely without brakes, except for the hand-brake in the guard's van. January 1962. (Author)

Exceptionally heavy rain in August 1961 caused an embankment on the West of England main line, at Patney & Chirton, to be washed away. A large number of the West of England main line services were diverted into the Bristol line, for a week or ten days, giving me a great time as a very enthusiastic young signalman. Here the flagship train of the Western Region, the 10.30 a.m. Paddington to Penzance, the Cornish Riviera Express, comes through behind 'Warship' class diesel No. 862 *Viking*. The diesel is carrying the curved headboard designed to fit on the front of a steam engine. Unfortunately the 'King' class steam engines were no longer working such heavy and prestigious trains when this was taken, from the window of Uffington box, on 16 August. (Author)

Relaying the Down main line at Uffington, entirely by hand, in September 1961. The crossover from Up to Down main runs out of the centre of the view. Note the GWR Down refuge siding GWR ringed arm signal. (Author)

Relaying by hand a half-mile length of the Down main line at Uffington. Ganger 'Butty' Martin can be recognised by his trademark trouser braces and cloth cap. To avoid inconvenience to passengers by forcing them out of the train to travel by bus, the railway used the procedure of 'Single Line Working'. This required railwaymen to stand out on the ground – in any weather at all for twelve hours through a night or day – to clamp points and handsignal trains. We did that without a qualm and were glad of the overtime. Four engines have been coupled together to form one train and thus get through the single-line section from Challow with much less delay than if they had to wait for each other to go through singly. They will cross back to the Down main a few yards further on. 1961. (Author)

They were a tempting sight, all those girls, as they came streaming out of the booking hall doorway on a bright morning and now that I was on my own I felt obliged to engage them in playful banter. I was surprised at the success I had in keeping a dozen of the prettiest around the base of the box, hanging, so it seemed, on my every word. We conversed with great gaiety – I was overwhelmed with my performance. Presently Les came out of his office. 'Thignal, thignal,' he lisped, 'ith the thopper about?'

'No, not yet, Leslie,' I replied in a nasty, patronising voice, 'not for a few minutes.'

'Well, whath thath one doing up there then?' pointing east towards Challow.

I had my back towards Challow and as I turned to look those wicked girls dissolved into helpless laughter, not sparing my feelings but even leaning against my signal box for support. There was the stopper, waiting patiently at the home signal which I had forgotten to lower in the excitement of attracting that horde of femininity. The signal was only 200 yards away, the driver *must* have seen the crowd of girls around the box, guessed I had forgotten him and kept quiet to see how long they could hold me up. Normally, if I had stopped him there, he would have played a symphony on the whistle.

An hour later the driver of the Faringdon was blowing long on the whistle for the branch home signal to be lowered as he brought the return trip up the short, sharp rise towards the station. I pulled lever 42 and went to the window to watch them round the curve. The little, black engine came cockily alongside the platform and, leaning over her cab-side, the driver and fireman were looking up at me with grins threatening to split their faces from ear to ear. They brought the train to a stand and came into the box to fill Knighton Crossing's drinking water cans.

'How about that then?' asked the driver proudly. 'She made it OK.'

'I should just about think she did – just. I was listening and heard you all the way to the top. You wouldn't have taken a single wagon extra.'

'Could you hear us when we were right up in the cutting?' asked the fireman incredulously.

'Not half, I could even hear when your mate let the lever down a notch.'

The driver grinned happily, 'She's a good engine …'

The guard came into the box then and broke into the conversation. 'You're a pair of mad blighters,' he said admiringly, 'we very nearly didn't make it.'

The driver did not catch his guard's tone correctly and thought he was going to have a row. 'What's up with you then? We made it, didn't we? And if we'd stalled, we could've split the train at the top of the bank and come back for the other half.'

'I don't know about the top of the bank – you very nearly split it at the bottom. I got such a jolt I thought you'd broken away.'

The driver's attitude changed immediately. 'Oh, didn't I have the couplings out tight? Sorry about that, mate. I was trying hard enough.'

'Aha! I could hear that all right and feel it too,' replied the guard. 'The cinders from your chimney were falling on the roof of my van like hail. I put my hand out and caught fistfuls but those wagons were so heavy that it was as much as your engine could do to move them, let alone accelerate 'em.'

'You cheeky beggar, she's a very good engine,' said the driver, pretending to be indignant. 'Ha! Ha! Do you remember when old Sid Gosling had a break-away out there and his van was running up and down for twenty minutes before it stopped?'

'Oh ah! He told me about it, said it was like being on a roller coaster and didn't want to spoil it by putting on the brakes.'

The driver continued the story. 'Yes, when the couplings broke he let his van roll back downhill and up almost into the station here and then off he went towards Faringdon. He did tell me how many times he came up the short slope before the wagons finally came to a stand, but I forget now.'

'Mind you, he was good, was old Sid,' said the guard in a tone of voice to indicate that Mr Gosling was not by nature a frivolous man. 'There was the time he had a break-away after coming out of the loop at Knighton. He didn't panic but let the wagons roll and managed to get them all the way to here, stopped just about outside the box. He steps out of his van, cool as you like, and calls up to old Walt Thomas, who was on duty, "All present and correct, Officer. Got the kettle on?"' We all laughed at that.

'Talking of kettles,' said the driver, 'how about getting one on for us then?'

Just before eleven o'clock the phone rang and I answered 'Uffington'. A roar of voices shouted a variety of greetings and abuse but gradually the noise subsided and Bill Mattingley asked, 'How are you getting on down there, Adrian?'

'Oh, very well, I think. The blokes on the Faringdon have been playing silly beggars with everything in the yard but it looks as if they've finished shunting now. It'd be nice if the passengers still ran on the branch so's we could have more shunting to do – better than just pulling off all day long.'

'Oho! He's keen,' someone shouted, 'we'll have to ...' A very nice-sounding female voice broke in with, 'Is everybody here? Anyone not present please speak up.'

'All here, ready and waiting, Margaret,' said Bill.

'OK now, standby ...' There was a long pause. 'Come on my duck, name the day,' said a Berkshire voice from somewhere. I heard muffled giggles and the sound of a dozen signalmen breathing into their mouthpieces. '*Time! Time! Time!*' yelled Margaret.

'Hurrah!' shouted the signalmen and telephones crashed onto their rests through the length of the Vale. 'Are you on here, Bill?' I asked puzzled. 'Whatever was that all about?'

'That was Margaret, the Didcot telephonist, giving the daily time signal for eleven o'clock.'

'Oh, I see. I thought it was a riot. I'd better get it written in the book.'

'Ah, but if you weren't actually watching your clock when she gave "Time" you don't know precisely how fast or slow your clock is. I'll give it to you now but tomorrow make an accurate check with Margaret, alter your clock if need be, wind it and put it all down in your train register.'

The men on the Faringdon signalled they were ready to leave at about 11.15 and a telephone call to Bill showed me that the Down line was free of trains – I had a time margin to get the goods to Ashbury loop. I pulled point levers 14 and 16, the ground signal to start them from the siding – 13 – the Down main starting signal number 4 and away they went; the little engine rasping merrily from her tall funnel, Knighton's drinking-water cans on her front buffer beam, a dozen wagons in tow, the driver playing tunes on the whistle till he was beyond the bridge. I watched the short train all the way along the embankment, curving slightly to the south, the Emett-like engine and her wagons silhouetted against the summer sky till they passed from view.

At half past one I was sweeping the box and tidying up for my relief when the phone rang. 'Hello, me boy. Going home time. Are you putting the duster round the shelves?'

'Hello, Bill. Yes, I'm ready to go too.'

'Tired are you? It's a lot different, isn't it, working the job for a full eight hours? Still, you'll get used to it; Uffington's a quiet little job. Do you know who's relieving you?'

'Well, Alfie White, I suppose?'

'No, he's got the afternoon off. You'll have Sid Tyler there at ten to two on the dot – call him "Brush", one of the best. Well, I'm off now. See you on the road home.' Bill's phone crashed down onto its rest before I could ask any questions.

I was at the end of the instrument shelf, near the window, just finishing the dusting when a tall, slim man in railway uniform and peaked cap, wearing reliefman's canvas leggings and carrying a canvas satchel over one shoulder, came strolling easily along the platform. He appeared to be about sixty years old, his face pale, lined and serious – my relief, I thought, and a bit of a misery too; old Bill was joking when he said to call him Brush.

I glanced at the clock as the box door opened – ten to two. Mr Tyler stepped inside, took the peak of his cap between his thumb and forefinger, tossed his headgear onto the coal box and with a peculiarly gentle smile said, 'How's yer Brush then?' I relaxed at once. 'All right, Sid, how's yours?'

'That's the style kid. Had a good morning? This is your first day, isn't it?'

'Yes. It's been very good. The men on the Faringdon livened it up and the girls going down to Swindon made a fool of me.'

'Getaway! What happened?' I told him as he took off his leggings, rolled up his sleeves and signed on in the register.

'Well I'm damned!' he exclaimed when I'd finished. 'They'd had it all planned, they'd seen you working with Elwyn – did you tell them you were going on the rules when you went down to Swindon the other day?'

'I told a girl from Challow.'

'Well, there you are then, they had that worked out for you. The railway's always good for a laugh. I've never regretted my time on it and I hope you'll never regret yours. They say you've always been keen on railway work.'

'Yes, but I missed five years of it by joining the Army when I left school.'

'Don't worry about it, kid. That did you the world of good and it gives us something in common, look ...' He pulled a wallet from his jacket pocket and, very gently, took two bits of yellowing paper out, put them on the register and unfolded them carefully.

One was his certificate as an instructor from the Army School of Signalling at Le Quensay dated 1917 and the other was his birth certificate. I read them both feeling excitement and awe. 'You were in the war as an instructor before you were seventeen, Sid?' He looked up from the papers; his eyes were blue and his hair – what was left of it – was fair. The lines on his face were caused by smiling rather than grimacing.

'I was fourteen and a half when I joined up,' he said in a matter-of-fact voice.

'Fourteen and a half!' I gasped. 'Whatever made you do it?'

'Well,' he said, with a half-laugh, 'a school pal, couple of years older than me, had joined and he came home with great big spurs on his boots and a big brass bugle – the glory of it was too much for me so I went to the recruiting office and told 'em I was nineteen. They didn't want to see birth certificates then; I was tall, they were hard up so they let me in. I was with the Wiltshires on the Somme before my seventeenth birthday.'

I looked at him with reverence, it showed and he changed the subject quickly. 'Here, you like railways – ever been over the old Tiddley Dyke?'

Still rather amazed, I said, 'No, I've never heard of it. Where does it run?'

'What? You never heard of the Piss 'n Vinegar, the dear old Milk and Soda Water? Oh! You've got a treat in store and if you're like me and enjoy the downland you'll have a double treat. I always look forward to a week in one o' them boxes.'

'Yes, but where is it then, Sid?'

'I'll tell you a rhyme so'll know how to find it – listen. When a parcel comes into Swindon Town station we Swindle it, we Chisel it, we 'Og it, we Mar it, we Save it, we Graft it, we Cull it, we Lug it, we Wey it and then we 'And it over.' He ticked off each station on his fingers as he spoke. 'Do you understand?' he asked.

His rhyme commemorated the old Midland & South Western Junction Railway stations at Swindon, Chiseldon, Ogbourne and on through to Andover Junction. 'Yes, I know the line a bit, I used to pass Grafton and Collingbourne on my way back to camp at Tidworth and Albert Stanley has mentioned the Old Town station to me.'

'That's it, old Albert did a lot on the Tiddley Dyke during the war. You go and have a close look round, talk to the blokes, you'll enjoy it.'

'OK then, Sid, I will. Thanks. Will you be here tomorrow?'

'No, kid, I'm down at Minety all the rest of the week but I'll hear from you sometime.'

I moved towards the door. 'All the best for now, Sid.'

'Keep yer brush up,' he called as I went out. I sank a little wearily into the seat of my Morris and drove home happy, even lightheaded, with a feeling of satisfaction; not even the recollection of the girls' ingenious leg-pull could sober me. I had carried out a busy shift – switching in, shunting, margining and straight pulling-off – successfully, apart from that isolated incident, which I promised myself would not happen again. I was very impressed with the gentle cheerfulness of Sid Tyler and looked forward to hearing more from him about the railway; but the greatest satisfaction of all was to be able to speak on equal terms with an engine driver, to be accepted by him as Officer in Charge and even as his equal. Work seemed to be a natural extension of the past fifteen years; tomorrow and for years ahead there would be shifts full of steam engines and admirable workmates. I sighed and settled deeper into my seat. I was part of the railway at last.

Signal Box
Standard Bell Codes 1960

Is Line Clear for?	*Head-code*	*Beats on Bell*
Express passenger train, newspaper train or breakdown train or snow plough going to clear the line or light engine going to assist a disabled train. Officer's special train not requiring to stop in section	A	4
Ordinary passenger train, mixed train or breakdown train not going to clear the line or loaded rail motor train	B	3-1
Branch passenger train (used only where authorised)	B	1-3
Branch goods train (used only where authorised)	–	1-2
Diesel rail bus	B	3-1-3
Parcels, fish, fruit, horse, livestock, meat, milk, pigeon or perishable train composed entirely of vehicles conforming to coaching stock requirements	C	1-3-1
Express freight, livestock, perishable or ballast train, pipe fitted throughout with the automatic brake operative on not less than half the vehicles	C	3-1-1
Empty coaching stock train not specially authorised to carry 'A' headcode	C	2-2-1
Express freight, livestock, perishable or ballast train partly fitted with the automatic brake operative on not less than one third of the vehicles	D	5

Express freight, livestock, perishable or ballast train party fitted with not less than four braked vehicles next to the engine and connected by the automatic brake pipe	E	1-2-2
Express freight, livestock, perishable or ballast train with a limited load of vehicles not fitted with the automatic brake, Weed killing train when spraying. 'Matisa' track recording car when not recoding	E	1-2-2
Express freight, livestock, perishable or ballast train not fitted with the automatic brake	F	3-2
Light engine or engines coupled	G	2-3
Engine with not more than two brake vans	G	1-1-3
Through freight or ballast train not running under 'C' 'D' 'E' or 'F' headcode	H	1-4
Lennox-Lomax earth auger machine, 'Matisa' or 'Plasser' automatic tamping machine not stopping in the section. 'Matisa' or 'Eliot' track recording car not stopping in the section	H	1-4
Mineral or empty wagons	J	4-1
Freight, mineral or ballast train stopping at intermediate stations	K	3
Freight, ballast, Officer's inspection special train, Lennox-Lomax earth auger machine, 'Matisa' of 'Plasser' automatic tamping machine requiring to stop in the section	H	2-2-3
Trolley requiring to go into or pass through tunnel	H	2-1-2
Train entering section	–	2
Out of gauge train which can pass another out of gauge train coming from the opposite direction	H	2-6-1
Out of gauge train which cannot be allowed to pass an out of gauge train of any description on opposite or adjoining lines between specified points	H	2-6-2

Out of gauge train which requires the opposite or adjoining line to be blocked between specified points	H	2-6-3
Opposite or adjoining line used in the same or opposite direction to be blocked for the passage of train conveying out of gauge load	–	1-2-6
Train approaching (where authorised)	–	1-2-1
Cancelling	–	3-5
Last train incorrectly described	–	5-3
Line clear to clearing point only (where authorised)	–	2-2-2
Warning acceptance (where authorised)	–	3-5-5
Line now clear for train to approach in accordance with Regulation 4	–	3-3-5
Train out of section, or, Obstruction removed	–	2-1
Blocking back inside home signal	–	2-4
Blocking back outside home signal	–	3-3
Blocking back for train already in section	–	1-2-3
Train or vehicles at a stand	–	3-3-4
Engine assisting in rear of train	–	2-2
Engine with one or two brake vans assisting in rear of train	–	2-3-1
Engine arrived	–	2-1-3
Train drawn back clear of section	–	3-2-3
Shunt train for following train to pass	–	1-5-5
Opening signal box	–	5-5-5
Closing signal box where section signal is locked by the block	–	5-5-7

Closing signal box where section signal is not locked by the block	–	7-5-5
Testing block bells and indicators	–	16
Shunting into forward section (where authorised)	–	3-3-2
Shunt withdrawn (where authorised)	–	8
Working in wrong direction (where authorised)	–	2-3-3
Train clear of section (where authorised)	–	5-2
Train withdrawn (where authorised)	–	2-5
Distant signal defective	–	8-2
Home signal defective	–	2-8

Emergency Bell Signals in Use 1960

Stop and Examine train	7 beats
Train passed without tail lamp	9 to box in advance
	4-5 to box in rear
Train Divided	5-5
Train or vehicles running away in right direction	4-5-5
Train or vehicles running away in wrong direction	2-5-5
Obstruction Danger	6
Train an unusually long time in section	6-2

Locomotive Headlamp Codes 1960

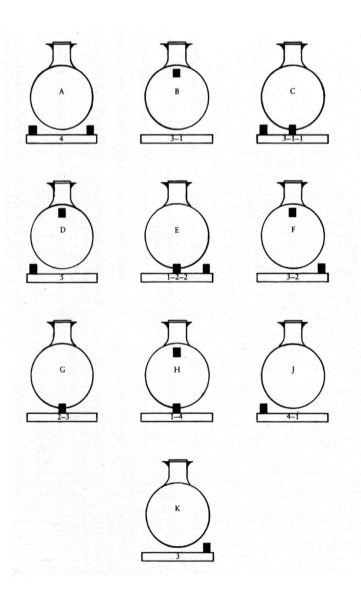

Appendix 4

Mainline Signals at Uffington

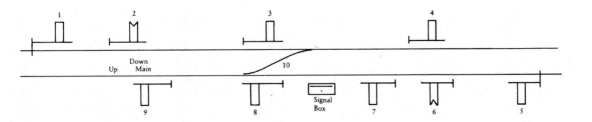

1. Challow's last Down line signal. Gives access to Uffington's section. The lever operating the arm is released electrically by Line Clear from Uffington.
2. Uffington's Down distant signal. The lever operating the arm is mechanically locked at 'Caution' until levers 3 and 4 have been pulled.
3. Down home signal. Gives access to Knighton Crossing's section. The lever operating the arm is released electrically by Line Clear from Uffington.
4. Down starting signal. Gives access to Knighton Crossing's section. The lever operating the arm is released electrically from Knighton's Line Clear indication.
5. Knighton Crossing's last Up line signal. Gives access to Uffington's section. The lever operating the arm is released electrically by Line Clear from Uffington.
6. Uffington's Up distant signal. The lever operating the arm is mechanically locked at 'Caution' until levers 7, 8 and 9 have been pulled.
7. Up home signal. Lever operating arm is mechanically locked at 'Danger' if lever 10 is pulled.
8. Up starting signal. Protects crossover. The lever operating the arm is interlocked with lever 10.
9. Up advanced starting signal. Gives access to Challow's section. Lever operating this arm is released electrically by Line Clear from Challow.
10. Main to main trailing crossover. When lever 10 is pulled levers 3, 7 and 8 are locked at Danger.

The symbol for the signal box is a rectangle representing the walls of the box. The line within the rectangle represents the lever frame and shows on which side of the box the levers stand. The dot represents the centre of the box from which mileages are measured, or, more picturesquely, the place where the signalman stands.

Index

ALSO AVAILABLE FROM AMBERLEY PUBLISHING

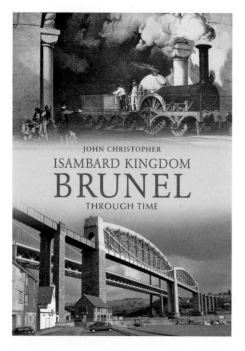

Isambard Kingdom Brunel Through Time
John Christopher

ISBN   978 1 84868 963 3
96 pages, full colour throughout

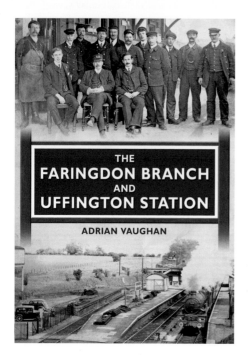

The Faringdon Branch and Uffington Station
Adrian Vaughan

ISBN   978 1 4456 0105 2
160 pages, 50 b&w illustrations